Cut from the Rushes

Cut from the Rushes

ANDREA BRADY

REALITY STREET

Published by
REALITY STREET
63 All Saints Street, Hastings, East Sussex TN34 3BN, UK
www.realitystreet.co.uk

First edition 2013
Copyright © Andrea Brady 2013. All rights reserved.
Cover image: "April 24, 25, & 26" by Nancy Prior

A catalogue record for this book is available from the British Library

ISBN: 978-1-874400-63-9

Earlier versions of some of these poems have appeared in *the baffler,
The Capilano Review, Chicago Review, Dusie, Edinburgh Review, Invisibly Tight,
Litter, Mute, The New Review of Literature, Notre Dame Review, Onedit,* the
Openned anthology, *Poetry Review, Ratapallax, Slope, Traverse, triquarterly,
The Wolf, Verse,* and *Yt Communications.* A translation by Matias Serra
Bradford of "A Following Sea" was published in *La Isla Tuerta*
(Lumeneditorial, 2009). "End of Days" was included in *The Wolf
Anthology* (ed. James Byrne). The anthology *Infinite Difference* (ed. Carrie
Etter) included "The Real and Ideal", "Still Hanging on Clinton's
Second Visit", "Cultural Affairs in Boston", "Fine-Line Ghazal" and
"End of Days". A German translation by Léonce W Lupette of "Saw
Fit" was published in *Schreibheft: Zeitschrift für Literatur 80.*

Poems with French translations by Pascal Poyet were published in
cipM 147 and can be heard at
http://www.cipmarseille.com/evenement_fiche.php?id=479.
Recordings of other performances are available online at Meshworks
(http://www.orgs.muohio.edu/meshworks/) and the Archive of the
Now (www.archiveofthenow.org), and have been broadcast on *Wordsalad.*

I am grateful to the producers of all these magazines and sites.

Embrace was published in 2005 by Object Permanence. Thanks to
Peter Manson and Robin Purves.

For Matt

EMBRACE

THE BALLOT SPOILERS

Don't fill up on that
junk the truth, a peppermint counter
dwindles from the ceiling over
our eyes and the scabbards of our throats;
snaps on the radio each equal
to a blanked kid, to every paper fed
head-side up down into slits.

You will recognise us by our
loyalty cards, as the lapwings do. We are
that class subscribed to postponing
resistance. We ride three minutes to midnight
arab bucks in the eventing. Justice also prances
along the medium line, leading with her right hoof.

If you unpack the paper carefully you will find it
is full of nails and metal but the image of shopping.
Charges dropped like a glass of water
knock about in upstairs gallery, may rise up
to the nozzle of retreating glaciers make climbers go
blind on a curve. It is their target
coupon, helps bulk the receipts a little.

How will I know what is dangerous, blown out
from surface by popping bags in freezer units, off
course burps of buttery spreads.
I have dreamed of you swinging
a rope with a concrete buckle, slinging it like
a hammer onto fields of china rabbits, many general
Swannacks ravening a walnut. In one hand,
she holds a basket of currency
things a person needs just to get by, pellets of
ethics packing peanuts. In the other electric
carving knife. You cast your shadows
over stable proxies, tactical voters frozen

in blocks with a floating appliance,
south of here lives get heavier

to form from so many chances like a stick of tallow
to force the choice stick in our blood   eyes
narrow under a bandana soaked in quinine. Our position
as permanent revolutionaries is waiting
by the pool for rustles in nettled
groundcover, for the uninterpretable blow
to make our coughing appetites fade
through films of oiled green, and disappear.

HONESTY

Only one head, not without its problems.

Shuffled sleep, waking the shoulder
somewhat better, quill of bone lies more quietly
against its blade. Spotted chests of a pair
look in here, into the escape pod, refer
narrowed like catseye catching
scent of expirations. Still one
prepared head, in which *una corda*
pedal strikes home two rubberised wires.

Between extra-nice and distant a shag
pile on, no little intensity, thicken personality.
With one head takes this one rest. Jolt
of pain on the intake, like a pierced
kidney, pinkish scapula. Ichor drips
down her acrylic claw. She tucks,
her hair, in the neck-brace, bunted
lip-shaped marks of foundation, then lies
down to wait for the next expansion
of the plastic diaphragm. Only one
will be coming.

A QUICK HALF IN THE SKINNER'S ARMS

I can see it growing on me   apexed
or just pointed   covering the head but not the
body   stirrup jar   baying
gliding slowly on the skin of
water   boarding   toward the head   grains
blowing over necks and beaks.
I continue to feel the shock   of the bite
in my tooth for another quarter   hour.

What is your body trying to tell
Trees are not in the same place they were
at morning, yellow extends its   reach
into the breaker's yard   Floral Passion
on my shins   after I dry myself, flecks of red
The men are much more vulnerable
Putting some cloth between me and dogs

Gave him a mohawk   Something
has to be found to suit   my
purposes   long and cylindrical   what is the point
it is a wing   calmly the eye rolls down the line
to the dog in the doorway   not that different
from what was seen   breasts flash their black tips
'the legal shop in any element'   tins her excesses
their hands blackened by powder   a 5 and a 6
on the backs of what look like   panel beaters

Still lust is a gap   intoxicant   hydrogen
passed in the presence of nickel   fat
becomes solid   spreadable   minute
changes in the atmosphere   a sigh breathed
out in agony girls   all look
the same curled and gold   boys
turning around on their mopeds to call to them
their hearts are beginning   to solidify   turks

reach for each other's necks   wrestlers
laughed at by the men in short order
skivvies   chestnut trees open   umbrellas of sweetness
there's an ecstatic feeling like a mouth
filled with water   I can hardly stand
it takes   a running jump onto a body
and the spasms   come and go

FROG LAB

This time it's thick with difference, wrapped
like a studded cushion under my ribs. I am separate
from hope, each little glass bell drying
on dish racks catches only light for hours
mostly eat somewhere else.
To make things difficult is to make the prospect
of transformation bright and perfect, treat over distance
fast as phenyl alcohol joins the air.
But that hope for kicks at picnics in
sunshine and cyclamen, two more matching
eyes flutters and zips
I stare it, it into abstraction. The pot on
the inspection chamber is now sealed.
Result turn up on a positive
or negative strip next week, if breathing
can just eventually get me
there. My pulse flatters time, gives it a name
when all it calibrates is indifference
and a few gutsy drops along the plotted nerve.
Something blue-black is seeping through hinges
the die-bold has been sharpened to a needle. Do I sit
with most hope as the absence of much doubt,
now that absolute certainty sounds like the intercom
batteries going slowly flat? We tried to invent
a troop the like of which
and with our failure nature goes dumb.
Now reach for the bottom of happiness
and smash up which cases around me, the outcomes
turn to this studied need in time, to learn
to make it stop or at least to kick in time to blinks.

LATER A SECOND VISIT

Yes that thing, the one   with the double tabs   your prize a blank
verse duped to sleeping   turning to face the window   where the light
is good for you   a rowan tree lowers its senses   toward the uncut
grass tips are crushed by setting   the risk management strategy
towards not asking   our brokers   every platter of jumbo shrimp tasted just
so tied her   hands to a stool   to keep her speaking   you were so
                                                    moving toward
the window even in the dark   I felt it right here   but like a field effect
transistor we kept working   the gate   as if the currents of joy's
enough reason   and impedance flashed on its gold
triangle   'what did you actually see in it'   'today'   'yes today'   pluck
names from the air   the engine kept running on the van
poised on new   York chicken   masts
bleating like frog eyes   money is now the blood
streaming through the firmament   gel I leave on the plastic
strip fencing   can we really hock even the interest
waves beat down the porcelain barrier   these are the flakes
that came off   the solstice sheet   no rumple lies I can
see Paul's and the domed burdens   which face returns
to its regulation third dimension   when the hazes shatter
like this country's acanthus leaves   in an ill wind   what burden
tightening the valves of the heart   so she cannot pull off
her risky investments   in a cloud of exhaust

TO CASTELLINA

Five globes, by these eyes. Where the lights
aren't so barren, archives open up their
substitutes are sugar out of which motion
flies into the corner of my eye

Has seen so many terrible things, as what flakes
in visible fear off skin and leaf, and now can
encircle them all in a riskless orbit
the little hole in the eye has exposed us

To nothing much redder than thread blows over
hand, cabbalistic witness to powers in numbers.
From furrow to usine, all they believe in us
our failure even to stop the balls from rolling

With impatience, back out to bramble making
songs of the expensive air by the station
it shook with waves. Loungers wait
for mama's boy to pluck their parallel straps.

Shift filled with an older body that has
its topmost turned outward, looks expecting
over humps of lettuce toward ridges
seen since moschus from looping ploughs. Lime

light and solvent like the water hoarding leaf,
or dark green favoured by a Senegalese guying
his concrete balcony into beer-flattened air. Who sees
patience navigates the gaps inefficiently, gasp caspar

implies another swell ruse of pink onlook
in swallowtail refit, hoarding wishfulness. Pink fudges
mountains like milk teeth or the anatomical line
of division and repetition which separates breast from breast.

Downtown chaos once seen disappears, degrading
map of people's insensible immemorial
no vision without pattern. My face now a sack
filled with a hot medical syrup.

The next stop skins up little golden hairs, swells with
handed paper for my face, air torn in my mouth.
The girls are patient now they are noticed, notches of skin
in their throats beating imperceptibly.

WIND UP

Wembley's white metal arch splits the household
cap from the circular, illuminate helix playing
fields against the estates. Through rain spatters on
drum skin here a coat of fantastic
lights gaping for all that space
between the arch and home. Night volumes
increase by up to 0.2 mm; skin that sweated
glucose kept her up into   bare
feet stubbed out little pyramids of salt she'd left
getting out of the dryer. Where was she,
iris a darkening slice. She won't
be drawn   a banner of foam that slowly detaches
as the gas falls down from her throat, assuming
a sitting position on her adjustable bed.
Corporal brown, orange and green resolving
on talkative hands, cupping the roll-up,
patterns strain to surface around the abscess
blown out of the head. The cramps return
during manned hours, charlie horse
again erasing past at the laundrette. Yr trucks
suck off the roadside's composure, hedges
favelas where the kids rule with tiny guns, try to walk
it off. Her fantasy requires brushing, the earth
near the border collar
set into unclosed rings, gravel out
the cyclist's thigh with wires. That is the seams
are there, showing up even
in medium violet   Even by the cold light
of an East River filled with skin.
To think she sat on
a deferral of conception, kindness to
herself slipped inside out. Hail of a drum
filled with cream burrs the outside
of the street   beads under the skin
shrapnel from roadworks. They are driving a new

route through into the unmapped
basin of Hertfordshire.   Children will
not watch spindles smoking in this light;
they have no memory of her as a young woman,
but the inside of a lip on their crown   the unclosed
ring which spills over their sleep.   Threw them
down the airshaft. Threw her cares
to the wind.

CHILD STARS ON TRIAL

Can you hear me? Over the trembling appliances
that coat fields of disprin and cherry, the tinkle
of a short lead. The child star's fist unwraps
around her lucky charm, on top of crinoline
transparency of a fag packet, empty, on top
of effusions like lemon curd. Knocked out, her reflexes
keep working the sack, corridors of her bones
shudder with the stupor of an electric handcart
bringing up more internal mail.

After about an hour of this I start to rumble,
prink the tarpaulin already wet and shiny
and try to heave her back down the blind passage.
Now you are all right, now repeat after me: she firms up
within the coffee clutch, perfumed by her gas supplier
the street's calmer for sleeping policeman, there is no
wainwright turning ash to the harness here,
no beasting corporal here to take pictures. Just
half a head over the firewall, some other she
must be stuck by hobs, thinking
nothing other than the rented video.

Hovering egg-tray taps in a minute polaroid
the noise of eggs nesting into plastic, into a vein.
Gone are the days of
a drop of blood in Brita water, oil of pear
for immunity, all singing all
like mescaline scored onto the writing table even silence
scored from end to end, pinned onto the empty faculty.

When she smoked in the shower, sweated
like a tennis ball on acrylic hotel duvets, and found
inviting the river below her toxic as pomade. So that it
could give up its sacrifice, deny the dented skin,
love ate temporarily against a wall of bridles and crops:

its owners are rolling back empty kegs over the Pont d'Alma,
echoing internally with fantastic shit-faced alternatives.

Then stopped on the greasy parquet
of the hotel of the city, sky doubtless like
mayonnaise, and all those gilt-headed creatures
open for inspection in her little fist. There is
no evidence. The waves panned out
like magnetic strips read by a chip, but the screen
saver says nothing more than welcome.
The barriers still stand, good
stable boys, letting the panels slip in
controlled outbursts should
the starring heart be occasionally roused to whisper.

FLIGHT DELAYED BY APPROXIMATELY

At the top of the berlin grain bin
a rectangle of white light, like a body slipping
out of bed still asleep. At the end of the year,
a forest of hard-edged trees, descaler
opening windows in snow. The background is
also catch to press, butts of kindling
blaze up to borders of whitewashed stones.

They make us take their pain in like smoke.
In another mirror my cheek puckers
like a lemon, best blister rotates under
the right eye. And it puffs out but not flat.
Smooth white barrel these muscles
like sea-dried rope up to the knees;
as I walk I lay red blunted hands on
hospice sheets, any horror
not too dramatic to the boys
working in dust at the top of the stack.

Sick to reset the past, and set it badly,
so the bone rebukes it. To bridle
the setter, get him to explore
tenderly the globes spinning under
my shingle bone, a ledger mashed down on
with little admissions. Even to bring
death in, reacquaint this unfired district.

Where the advocates stalk time, catching the cross
town breeze off standing pools when afternoon
sun makes them vibrate with new life.
Who will stop for me? A lobby
shop for today's shine boy. A bar for sweet
children looking less like we raised them.
The hardest 'yes' for the last one, the gull
snacking furthest out, riding the swells.

BUILDING SITE

It was easier for the mouth than laughing better
exercise for the temporarium,
though planks got stuck and exhaled drafts
and soaped now, with the unbuttoning of your skin.
So your fingers slip out of gloves as the leads'
bodies drop into the city crevasse – their joy cannot be
imagined as they pass floors 40 through 30.   Not put out
by the cone, we would not be put out by the blinding
light. Shines a filament of pure silver nerve from each
currier queuing in front of the forge. They're gorgeous,
kind of social, gone wild with follies. Badged and in blue
wigs, agents of desire slip colour to them in fuchsia pills
until dawn wakes up the sponsor's big screen.

    When even a doorway must be muscular, a bank
slash hotel bulbous and vulgar as the railroad
man's image in three quarters mirror,
the blank side rufous and absorbent of the street,

        it's up to the likes of you
        to coin a strategy
        to stay awake.
        Blinding light gives way
to nights deep as the one continuous sea hemming
your bit by bit houses, air counterpane
perpendicular to wants driven home
a sink of unpaved water.
Take cone from shelf, place
over head, and bang against
the boards as you sleep, two by
two. You can still feel the warmth of a body in the water
though it is passing you quickly, whisked into foam.
Your dream of forcing the ground back
as that wild drop is condensed into inches, is bred
in the tanned basket of your groin, that
body stripped becomes a bow, colour of a gram of milk,
wild as it retreats under cover. The light

of its nerve writes silver
initials on air only you can see. Your place is marked
by two bow-shaped metal handles,
here your lunch is, here you irradiated with news aspire
as a low whisks your frock, turned up
like tulip bow to wind, your face turned
up to a cloudy nylon that makes the blue work
against it deep as a container port. Not like beams
chucked up, rusted, torn down, chucked
into parallel lines in yards, dispersing
into a medley of ironic dots, but like air
under which the rocks grind. You grind your face up. You spark.

THESE THINGS HAPPEN IN OUR HOMES

Toyle to prevent imaginary wants
who calls on me with her human voice
and when she rang it was a cashback
offer on the female intrusive cancers.
Who lack a birdbath are covered by the sky,
that self same
bevelled strap to   muse yourself on
The great dictator an interesting rhetorical figure,
weeds tickling between the ribs rock
the whole hat-stand with chortles, bugs
run out of   sky as historically conceived

delivers a series of bad eggs we were born out of
to which is calibrated every instrument.
The lads are testing with four near-perfect
spheres the potential for relative warps
In a clean way, the dragging of space into motion
Microdancers latest crazy child
a second educated detail
marked off like the face of a clock.

Well he *was* beaten to death but he was not a man.
More like a jack fruit, opened by razor
and held browning in styrofoam   up-country
games for hunters   on ice   skates took   Boredom
drives me, forceps, and desire
seen here in my knickers   The till lady says
'my loved one' to Peter with a fistful
of change beside her   a third of us hostile,
arbitrary and inventive
jawing through the fuselage

The cropped girl in the camel-bone mirror
does not have on her face
that she will soon discover herself to be a mother
She hikes in on an ass in a hail of
curses   she hock-crow eating her
up inside   it was harder than we expected.
It was more abhorrent than we expected, more ...gushy.
Don't even *like* gays, what they do in their own homes.
Opposition gets harder, lacing up
the eyeholes of the dead with TV

tubes. If these things can be comprehended,
you're fucking orbit, air apparent, your fire engine lip
sticks   cover the trap   sealed with organic resin
of as-yet-unknown origin. Want to hurtle across the sky?
The dark gets to, and cold rushes up your bevelled edge.
If not, and you *lie*, then heaven help you
down from the optional gothic panorama. You curl up like
pellets in your loading bays. The whole will open up to you
as the trap clicks through each of its twelve stations.

THE BOXER

The inspectors supply precise heat to pierce
a vein stem, thread a match head
recoding its will to light.
Our veins like cylindrical seals
are wrapped up in their own
staggered figures, flashes and burnings
from a prehistory of growth and trade.
Hunger and fullness fuses those double pithos
buried into shapes of tongues, fallen in the cold
wars sleep shoulder to shoulder.

Steam in a hairdresser's window shaped like head
stones. They fry what comes out of our head,
which we have been growing for days into an environment
of noise. Between splints
organs struggle to move and do their jobs,
blast the body with precise heat. We age
in a display case, feeling the stub
and sometimes greasing the knot with texts;
a verbal clock gets hung up on
the studio wall, limiting the interview
until the last word abdicates to space
finally leaving each of us alone.

Mineral sky pulverising the sea like
what the body was doing bowed before it,
framed by flagpoles, docked life
boat tack laid out for arraignment. Waiting for
the mass to generate its own heat, though each
aspect may reduce and grow cold, we know to expect
a man in a suit, under which, red silk trunks.
While in North Korea we found   time
to resume talks and untold figures
shot through with red, welt these free airs.
Inside it is an organ also looking like it has
something alive inside it, a foetus, or a hare in a bag.

HOW MUCH TO HAVE A GO

to attract   flies. I take home
some ocular proof, lie it like celluloid strips
to drip from poplar racking, then rest my face
before the open musical door,
watching the fatty street for foxes,
watching the slideshow of temps unaware.

She was docked a time
out by her father, she's been taking
snaps by rule to develop in a red light
tears to the eye   Adders set on us
in the cot, stags blocking the
stairwell, what chance do we have
a go at the fair bruiser on his stiff coil,
asking for more with that apple-red cheek.
Any gift is the surplus of a repudiation;
when you've done your time, you fly into
conditions not fit to raise a tempest in.

So the link collapses like an old story
after wearing into a hook then a
wire   Then powder drops out
of the air, outlining a man on the ground. We can go
on   splinters of horn nailed right into
green trees   where they fought against nature,
get bundles of light to tell
us where we went
wrong, downhill out of sight
past all minding. When the memory rises
like a spring   flight or
fight – those two hard splits – flow again
into the jam of tissues and knots. They flash
like city blocks,
rain braces burnt sky for its dressings.

ARNICA MONTANA

                on the way home.
Collect the provings in a cruet, stopped
the tip with baking paper. Struck on the thigh
with a crutch   lashed into a love of thirst.
Defeated cells act like bilge traps,
yellow prime swells with poison,
pushing forward acceleration rinses the chassis.

My sisters call their mountains, their hind
sight a regional city calcifying above the rock base.
They are the intercept, our bond an aegrotat
certificate: gravel up to and smudging on the bottom
and sides of them, uncut columns, drawing life
a report crusting their feet. Right the safety
launch and float tiring, still without distress
a marrow on a salty surface. Or hooked over
and pulled through and flipped on the back
like a spring-loaded belly. But if we're being

bruising already spread into the occupied quarter.
What can't be put on, pulled over. Hit from below,
vertigo blooms from the cold pockets, renumbers
each 'safe for human' interstice. These are ours
bonds lined with suede. Focus the search
on the pins drifting along that particular outflow:
there are they now, dripping on lamb's lettuce, falling,
choking among rocks. What are they made of?
A purse of the old war

wound retreats into clips made of mange
and the final kicking of four legs, months stuff
themselves on devilled eggs at the resort sideboard.
Then a bolt could be seen as colour returned all
along the fleshy part, up to the eye gash
where blinks coded its deep thirst. If it quacks like a

get to the bottom, thresh the stalky surplus
they wait, compression floods their brains with angels.
The tapered head of an unknown creature
struggles against the current, down by the groynes,
up here all is clouded with factor 15
shine. Say to her, the purple will quiet down

IDEAL HOUSE

Den of dusty bobbins, awls and bores: who
is looking for it? A girl lip
bottled her red lolly – swelling up – fingers the belly
slopping over her ra ra, eye-curl uncurling. Caught
shells on polyolefin wire, watched them, Serbs sucked
out the tin cross-links in Hellshore rooms.
You will see some things here

the jittery bird punches light over our studios,
jittery and obvious whipping the air. Push gas
pedals down, also seek gently to release the clutch,
trouble won't stay gobsmacked on the traffic island behind you
for long one follows with a bike and tv in hand, giving you
the option. Inside your ears, cellos
and the panic of blades losing their grip on nothing

gut ship may be going up or down or sideways it's impossible
to plot without a marker. You just wait
for the conveyor's tyrannical grunt
finally coughs up a calendar of oil from further
downtown the track, barrels gouged with carbuncular
blame on you. It comes out of the east like your death
instinct warns, 'should not be loose
shunted'. The hairline scratches. One
hump and the catalogue of houses
all are ablaze, dooms a panned Russian landscape.

The girl from above opens her mouth: 'I have taken
everything' she knows what she means. I see myself
shunting around that idea, which lights
the asphalt slapped by terrorist feet
doesn't give   with ideal shadows. All along
you think you're at work finding a true pleater.
And are also tracked
across the northern line.

HYMN ON THE NATIVITY

The place went silent. You could hear
my jointed name heated sachets expand in arches
as Cadillacs stretch towards Olney, the whole detail
dripping on a lace-edged runner purled
to the edges of banked leaves. Over the top
of smoke unbundled like measuring tape,
a sliding hatch clicked eight times
caught the lip of the shuttle and dragged back, like
fire picking its way through a beaded curtain.
In the quiet night you lay down on lawn.
You were not with me, but your fingers
stuck out through packing foam when you
woke, tipping over with their soft pads.
Your name jointed in the half-glow of the forecast
sprinkles a tough crunch, catches the lattice
and almost makes it to the house.

Toys pivot on branches cranked up
toward the stars, poised in their seasonal life
turned out by the little impostor; I begin to
am giving you that's a first our life
to mount from here in reverse cascade. On ledges
metal icicles attribute to the candied light. Hard
as the hardware is nothing can be used much more
than these beacons already are. Some packets lay on top
of the cotton set out for you
to put between gum and lip. But nothing
goes totally silent, even potted water
when the animals pause, looking at our flesh
becomes clear and dark, a painted rattle at the bottom of it.
Fishnets of diamonds drop out of the air,
fall and melt, so it's still alive and gripped,
bent on acquiring a few planetary accessories not on the rope.
The surveyed ground to a firm space, against
our most destructive wishes for patience,

to wait in the dark of the captivity for a long and wistful sentence.

Yours is like no life I have ever lived, and now
steams through the dismantled grate a poultice of ginger.
What do I really need, my old seasonal question,
lives together flexing the temper even trees skirted.
Tuck cold behind a sheaf of rubber, tuck your chest
under feather, and myself sleeps in your mouth.
All I have incurred so much more I have
to say before they lower their heads, all yours.

SWING STATE

        Melts down the base of street
        furniture, those lemon vests
        whose work my lungs reject
they make the night air swarm with asbestos and crystal.
They light deals on the pitch and brush
back the fringes of commerce, how they plough silence
up from lower strata. Preparing to punch out
on the switch that stops the auto
destruct mechanism, as their ship spins back toward a desert
planet, cooed by that calm numerate lady.
Nothing comes up over a few mugs.

You have been told not to stand under the tipping body.
Follow along the gantry and let down the gauge chain.
Topped off a swag cradle at 65 kilos, lower down
into the hot oil puckering beside that needed switch.
The cold snatch some flames thence, the valiant more
flashes and then the outline of a little fist, done in charcoal.
What might the snake achieve by caution, or the biting dog.
Where do we look for, the telltale twitch in our enemy's
shoulders proclaims the haymaker's

coming? Animals rattle over cardboard, a red sub
rises out of the carpet's regency paisley, blood
flickers like a drippy burner trying to circuit the whole
contact plate. The announcement
is simple, grinds down on a button. A swift
launch into the jungle is our faintest hope.

Laying another few miles
lying down in cotton busy with life
measured in millimetres. Never a rising.
Nothing ever explodes with mirth or rage
among the white grades where nothing
gets made. When the sequence

gets to zero it is set to go
straight back to 100
rivets pop out like shrapnel as we
career toward molten dust. And for the dead
there will be bottled water and biscuits.

MASS HYSTERIA AT THE ROYAL FREE

You swore by the fringe of the tractor shed
to be careful. Taking your companion
by the neck by the shirt skimmed her like a sail.

She is dressed in comparisons,
powdered help circulates above her head.
Between the rods in the fist flesh can go
white   a container like these
lofts towards Harlesden force sky
white as treacle-streaked shaving foam
into the prerequisite unmanageable depth.

After hefting cartons of milk went on
break   lifting arms still pinioned to the sun.
Up there the rent opened and dropped
on the broads and turning spaces its heating
benefit for old birds. The hash on
the shed's keypad got warm: soot burns at least
twice on a neck. Snap of fowler's thumb.
The whole can change become
a spoon of vivid emerald liquor.

How are the accounting girls supposed to write up
these expenses? Chips to that stupid extra
tea set, holes the size of knuckles around
the loading dock. Lie still and rest so
the incisions stay thinner The infant who pulled down
a curling iron onto her cheek still cannot speak.
Shouted for my trainers, which she brought quickly;
does she sleep scabbed in a top-knot,
always running through forests of waxy fir.

Cold came off the man standing in
the doorway, packed temper in wool.
How long did you last, your desire

to outrun cut perspex in open space
really snap like an inadvertent wing. All are
wound up in their trundles, anger is theirs
battery makes machine men crawl noisily
across the rug. We hear the repeats
raging through the brickwork. Is it enough reason
She lies there hearing everything:
the peacemaker's whine, the sonic bust
of an absolute will to make her move those
actually good limbs, get up from that little rest.

WORKSITIN

A mid-morning package on
how to cut wood with
swords. We come a froth
of cold over the prompter, you lap us
up. Are you still going cadaverous
with over work? I see you
have dispatched linguists into
the warrens, dried in ticker-tape,
the good platinum of two thousand
hung in their throats on lubricated wire.
Our dinners are themselves
humps of warm orange under park
benches, and no amount of air
will clean the sick coils beginning to breed
in each octagon of skin. Dust and electric
green rakes our public discourse for metal;
anything magnetized will come out. A trill
vibration in the rinds of a truckload
of smokies calls for you to understand socialism,
the call resounds through flaps of heart still stuck
to the racket of christian ribs. Can't you hear
your own helium death rattle, like a rivet
as he shuffles his body for the last time
closer to the plaster? If I swell infested with pity
toward the relics of solidarity, the warm body
where djs spin our confusions into a social need,
us there together, you are in the way my mouth
works, distributing possible syntax down a mains cable.
You are ruining the idea of love, running out
into streets made more technical than gas;
and I cannot check you with my palmer's rod,
or even by splitting my throat into curtains
around a shadow play of lepers and skinned hares.
I see another morning with the spectrum
blotted by an asymmetrical panel of gauze into a finish

of grey, and eyes that don't have time to be
iconic sold into history under Gerhard Richter's lacquer.
We are running out and what you don't know is
hurting us at the exit, a cavity split from the groin
to the lips by an industrial mower.
The hawk you are listening to was once a baby
blistered with milk, you could have finished it then
without leaving so many chunks on the patio.
Between us and ponds and tenderness is a field
of razors, programmed to tilt
towards our houses whenever we call
out, alone together, in the panics of absolute need.
The airs play over the serried information you give us
tap us like unbonded wood, sanded with
our own teeth. Yes we have had more than enough.

MY FLESH AND BLOOD

The heart is dribbled ever closer to the parquet
by fear of loss, the heights it reaches
in mimicry of the speaker that has lost all
her children only so high
as a safe identification: it will not beat
itself as fast as all of them, to death.

At this moment exists only in language
we wait for a promise, another genus feature.
But why are we waiting. Like pickers stolen
from fields of citronella, we are aghast
dropped from our empty chore and so
insects burn a little less. The evidence

uncovered is a treadmill of animal
bones riveting the sand. We wait
to give ourselves up
to disaster for a pass
word, type, turn over life
like a barrel of nothing,
for running burnt tar to Next.
This text makes a filthy lining
stuck to the bus shelter, sponged
out of the sink of his mouth. No body has

a pulse so regular you can set the sun by her
current account of blood ebbs under the thin
carpet of waiting rooms. The patients aghast
but the flow is regular. What else is alive,
how many more forces can we commit
to make the abstract nouns ring out over
confused territories where this is the energy
released by our needs. I am expecting
my answer, like a twin grown on me for science,
to be delivered and thrown out.

TABLE TALK

So many excluded in a quick pinch
a little rain of lemon bitters down the back of you
but complex jawing just sets the compression
programme to rerun from its first sector.
How can we be different.

Could I make it any simpler? Put the bumper up to
the spill kit to avoid the rain. Pump four
covered in swallows, return to a query easily
programmed: I think there's a drying
rack. Oh, drying rack? Say it politely
the sheep's skull must have cracked
when it plunged onto the strand from the pasture.
How much is that. How cool. Calling
the police in the morning, the shore strafed
with wool, not drowned or removed at night who
takes all out past the twelve-mile mantle
of national waters into the spell deep.
All your possessions, What show is that.

Asleep in a pile of coats in the back
bedroom while the adults drink. Is it
expensive. Say that again slower.
Nudged by hunger to the shelf-edge
gorse, and so removed. To powers of iridology
raise the living and blind at well spring. Non's boy
grew to spend days in a mortification of cold water,
tempering his loudest desires. I paid good money

for that is now plain mutton, leg ironed flat alongside
its companion, cold bullet of seal. Two empty eyes up,
refusing to be drawn. At the semi-formal you found
something to say as you were drawn like a fish
along the receiving line, up to the cool hand
of the principal. Is it love. Your three-minute warning is

up close with the swallows, taming the night
above a midden of. Unspeakable desires hold
their pattern full of suet and liver, sauce
that provocative thought in its cavity. Know better to talk
nice to the others who dote on
flat spaces, go all the way to a bulge in the sky.

ANOTHER NOISE BAND

At the practice session, Charlton Heston
subs for the voice of God urging the branch

Davidians to surrender. All the nonlethal components
are here, sticky foam, flying nets, saunas,

a metal box filled with slush, urine on the brush,
nakedness, cheerleaders, sergeants who pull hair,

18 months alone with a camera. Shelled and lacerated
by surplus tactics, the division's scruples bed down

with termites, make shipping containers seem so funny
far from any bay. Even "the Roof Is On Fire" gets

playtime in the new metal version. Next they'll be slaughtering
bunnies, or flicking the air-conditioned cortex with a rotor.

What do you know, these morals are a tight fit, an
RPG through a bolt-hole, down in the burrow

pink eyes twitch. What creates the mood better for snipers
than free improv? Rap tracks the dune gangsters,

hot jazz makes counted eyelids blink. The pursuit of truth
threatens to split his brain on a rim. The centre

is a place where Norah Jones gets played
and so do the citizens by a whorish martial duo.

Everybody in Little Rock make some noise. Show them we
can drop dead on time, sickened by the food of love we eat

with corps djs spurting industrial noises from the temples,
compressed air and horses eating each other all night,

that centrally heated night we've been keeping for whispers
of love is a rump in bed with Kris Kristofferson.

AMMONIA CRISPS THE AIR

When the wind changes though it
didn't change my heart
slipped like a marble into a slot,
toddles there even now in a cup of magnets.
This pause feels giddy, as it drops
and flattens its glossy coat on all the visible hills.
Can that smoking patch return to cadmium yellow
so hopeful it burns the back of the throat, can it
be soul, ripening in the unbound sun?
A body in love in a cab is poised, brisk,
gathering to shout or stretch
arms straight into the air.

That lot's brought back by ammonia
drips on a fitting head. The anorexics at the bar
examine the options, plead stress and celebrate
wins laughing among themselves. In an economy of cordial
we listen for help in catastrophe,
what the scabs will pull over next – iron and leather,
or in our honour, peace and peace.

Do we recognise the name they just gave us,
do their identikit materials return some trust?
Jolts over the points
scare us into stretching for a fur-covered buckle
but may be nothing more than the fitful reprieve of metals
on which all this life imports. Sometimes the phone rings,
and then we hear smoke, binding us in electric flux
to the national grid. The crawler lane will be filled
with enemies of the people watching
your cut-and-shut motor for signs of fracture for the next
hundred years: by no means pull over,
even if your leniency is ready to drop.

Sure behind her blanket of bandit proof
glass the teller may not want back talk
how figures for bonds and securities
give early birds the green sickness, the economy
shriven by spending on rough linen covers
always on the verge of collapse. She knows that
muzzling under bark is just a tapenade
of beetles, inside the presidents
are wrapped in tab-top muslin
and ready for eternity.

Our time rent with chips and pins surrenders
only something of its general drift, our
rest stops on the slide in a mutiny of floral notes.
When the long night beats like a propeller
on the blinds of Pentonville, our thoughts
are boxy, big and capable. The single person acts
elbow-up on the naked socket
of a battery terminal, when she is cinched by the ear.

DISAPPOINTMENT

You cannot know what you have wanted,
but you will not get it.
Stains that run down to the transco scar show
how leaves, your bullet-pointed trapezes, burn out like
stock cars and the final sequence, when his hand gets caught
under an industrial door or in a hamper of dry ice.
The city moves them on with industrial air. Switch off.
But these scars are the wagoner's design for the future,
not a set of summer weeks that took direct hits from the lamps.
How could you recognise the coast from these drawings,
converted rectangles plumped with numerical code?
You're being sent someplace different, where the men
descended from the northerners, by their hands over time
retracting into claws. Don't worry, they are safer
they cannot work the little pistils from the heads.
Toast your future, a corroded metal split into bad coin.
You won't be able to use it to pay for conversation,
now that you've smiled through your hour in the dock; all talk
of certainty is through the tack-chamber, your back rigged
with magnets and a gallon of milk. You are again through.

A kind life teetered on each of those states, and drove
through the gaps of your imagination are detached pairs
of leggings, and boxes of seventies party games.
You who have consumed everything but the fuse cannot
light your insides with an outdoor extension, unless
you wrap it around your knees, doubled with telephone cords
you might switch on the Pentecostalist's tongues of flame.
Talk to him. Switch off. The glass bone is filled with corrosive
liquor, lights down, moths waiting in their most recent
cluster for it to shatter. This will be you as patron
of hope: a seamstress, blinded by justice,
future snapped like cheap thread. It isn't all
transport, your nervous system, though you might think
that your life rolls away from your mechanical body

in gobbets of acrylic, latex, basic shitty brown.
They are wrapping their promises tighter around their
spools, with each biscuit parade you end up slapping
your shins against grit that smells like incense and lemonade,
but you feel better, because you will feel less, next time
on point. So come home to the plants, to the surfaces
polished under the bridal sleeve, and serve
up your ration of beef cake and Budweiser, to dirty
the cracks in your heart: down to the grip. You are allowed one
trip to the bath room, to give it your best shot,
the plunger massaging your throat's ethical knot. Begin
again switch off: lay off the
winter outfits with that creeping rust
stain of disappointment, your body will get older, your head
sequestered in its tightening bag of skin.

3.11.04

ALL OR NOTHING

What is right? Combinations snag on the drift of Paradise
city farm, receding back into clouds
of exchange unless kept up, or kept in
the coal hole, to waste like an old fashioned compact.
The Virgin conductor's key set to inhibit
or enable   flaps the handicap autonomically
down.   Outside, rangers dropped off by
a sports authority   clangless in their keds
grow up to the ramp of the community
association where they sick up. Can be seen
a woman in the scruff, catching a puff
off the junkies bothering their red stripe and her:
you see you   I am there too. When this group leaves, nothing
will be all ready. What is right, if right
is disused and skeletal, a surplus of spoken
labour hunkered down in rough?

Why not she, or you speak again like a pro
weighing the projects of the whole from boss
to serfs drag back a ravelling rope as one
always can do. You there, both, slap your brands
on cows and dogs shitting up this place noiselessly.
Even as you feed them triscuits in neglect
they feel green shade slide past them like a verb:
right this. Then go as the soldiers do, live actors,
driving nails through a little syllable. That you are not yet
right in the head does not mean that you will be killed off.

To view source, without frames, the user must
hey get up, perk up, you can sure walk.
Speak to us about your dreams. My gusset
had been ripped out,
though the rest of the legs were just fine,
and as I could say that I remember this I wake
the boy boiled in pig-iron bobs from colon to throat.

With that spell we are driven out into the street
and dragged half way along under all manner of signs.
Was I right, was I, would otherwise drift
back down an open gullet and trade the rest
for a magic chip pumped with human song.
Like the secret of the human ears
if I gave up my own tongue, I for that matter.

TO BE CONTINUED

I've been waiting for you all
night, a half-crescent uncovered and brought
to bear in a theatre of scriptless desires –
how winged you, your thirties in code
dragged up to an audible pitch, intent
on not to switch off for the rest of the sequence.
That life of credit, heated room in which to be
brought to bed, played out and down in ecstatic
the person asleep, inside, be
side with dreams fabulous in their modest outfit.
Having weighted the alternatives, what does it
matter spilling out of an overfed barrow
if this explicit and unmistaking you
for anyone else is less than perfect, cannot be
there at the receiving end, this calibrated instrument
still shuddering with the alert notice; not too heavy,
not too individuated, your face the sun up
ends the world with racing stripes
run north to south like a tie to countries
and to all imperfect people we might still be.
You are already awake. Now that does it
fit seems exact and entire surrounding, you will
continue running through the tone a blade
of white and silver streamer, so gorgeous
a hush falls down
the fault of language.

CAUGHT

Behind the baize door fields doze
sticky dancers tether themselves to painted horses
tire   slowly   only over the whole panel
behind them   cut with their compulsions.
And behind that   hatched collects
of ash break apart the white spectrum   and what rain
will fall out of the stream like honey
sung thin as cooped hair   hoovered from
the islands, behind them   shelves of ice and metal.
Sirens open up rented quiet   humming
and creaking trade of what flies with what
stays   sucking the ground   so do cars
with the seven sisters twisting in their hatch,
and the god-bothering sick ones   and leaves
showing their pale frontage to the tropical remnant.
Even their carrion crew   stapling dust to jackets
which sling metal into cemented post houses   files
into order   of a rapid impeded plenty.
Though a kid seethes in milk   and boys spit
on the roster   and the dirty bag is wailing below
I can only be reached carefully, hanging out
at the greyhound station   Waiting to trim
cuffs the impossible   with bosco honey.
Behind a new panel slid in from the channel
opens a window: the keyhole cut reveals not
aligned nerve   I see nothing
but a blaze of pure gold   At this rare
appearance the turnstile
puckers in its chest: that we are caught behind
and blinking, when our lives together could swarm
love all over the grid.

MONTANI SEMPER LIBERI. ALL OF HEAVEN A BIT
SKELETONS. THE UNHAPPY MEMORY OF SCALPIN(
SOCIAL, CULTURAL OR INDUSTRIAL PROGRESS TO BI
FESTIVAL IN RICHWOOD; HE WORKED AT THE PR
POCAHANTAS CO., INVENTED THE CHAIN-STITCH
REVOLUTION. BLUE GRASS. HER SEVEN STURDY S(
SULPHUR RESORT. HER UNCLES MADE ELECTRICAL I
SANDSTONE, SUITABLE FOR EVERY PURPOSE. REHAI
RODE HIS HORSE OFF A STEEP CLIFF. THEY CALLED I
WERE NEVER STRONGER OR MORE DETERMINED: '
YOUTH WAS NEVER MORE URGENT. GOLDEN CIN
"ABORIGINAL ARABS OF AMERICA". GRASS OF PARN/
BY THE WEIRTON STEEL COMPANY. KNOWN HENCI
REFRIGERATOR. 'MAGIC VALLEY', THE NATION'S CH
CUT-OVER TIMBERLAND. THE TWINKLING LIGHTS (
TANGY WILD GINGER. THEN OF COURSE, THERE IS '
FESTIVAL IN OCTOBER. BLUE CHICORY GROWS
DODDRIDGE COUNTY RESPONSIBLE FOR THE GREA
OF ICED CLOUD OVER HIS FROWNING. A FURRINER
SUGAR MAPLES AND ATE THE GOODNESS WITH :
"SUNRISE" WILL BECOME THE PROPERTY OF THE
HOMELESS WAIFS. MADE BLUING. THE BLUEFIELD (
FREE LEMONADE TO ALL-COMERS WHEN THE TEMP
WHERE THE WAKEROBIN GROWS. MADE COIN NICK
AND A GREATER STATE. WATER WHICH THE INDIAN
CURIOSITY TO CEASE EXISTENCE. MADE CHLORINI
LAST BISON KILLED AT MOUTH OF TYGARTS VA
CONGRESSMAN FROM THE 6TH DISTRICT, GRAND C
MASON AND SHRINER, INDEPENDENT ORDER OF
MOOSE. PETROLEUM-BEARING SANDS. FRATERNITY
BOZARTH, ARMED ONLY WITH AN AXE, KILLED THRI
LARGEST ONE-PIECE RUG IN THE WORLD. THE TIMI
WHEN THEY STOP PUMPING SEWAGE INTO BIG SAN]
100,000 SPECIMENS OF PLANTS, FILED UNDER FIRE-PR
SLOW OF SPEECH YET CURSING FLUENTLY TO PAD
IDEAS OF HIS FATHERS. LIFE TRULY WAS IN THE RAW
CINDERELLA OF THE APPLE KINGDOM. CRADLE ST/

BELOW WHICH, A WALNUT VAULT CONTAINING FIVE
URES, PILLAGE AND DESTRUCTION. NO IMPRINT OF
N HIS TRAIL. THEY MET AT THE SPUD AND SPLINTER
Y REMEDIES COMPANY. E. A. GIBBS OF MILLPOINT,
MACHINE. BLUE CHICORY. BACK DOOR OF THE
OW DOGTOOTH VIOLET GROWING AT THE WHITE
N. GOVERNOR DINWIDDIE SUGGESTED "VANDALIA".
SPIRITUALLY AND SOCIALLY UNDER ITS INFLUENCE.
V, THE WEST VIRGINIA BANANA. THE FORCES OF EVIL
FOR "LIFE GUARDS" TO SHIELD AND PROTECT THE
. FROM THE MOUTH OF KANAWHA ROAMED THE
-PYE WEED IN WEIRTON, A TOWN WHOLLY OWNED
S MCCOLLOCH'S LEAP. WONDERS OF THE NATURAL
ENTRE. STALKED IN THE MATTED UNDERBRUSH OF
EET GLASS PLANT AND AXE FACTORY, CHARLESTON.
T VIRGINIAN OF SUBSTANCE. DANCED AT THE BIBLE
THE VITORLITE PLANT. AN ARTIST-FARMER OF
HE BEETLING HEIGHTS OF SPRUCE KNOB, A MANTLE
HMAN. STALKED THE BAY LYNX. STUCK PLUGS INTO
LLOWING THE PASSING OF THE PRESENT OWNER,
N ARMY, IT IS SAID. A LARGE SUMMER CAMP FOR
OF COMMERCE HAS A STANDING OFFER TO SERVE
REACHES 90 DEGREES, PLUS. SETTLED AT TUG FORK
MORE SCOUTS, THE FEWER JUVENILE DELINQUENTS
T AFIRE. DRILLING OF SALT WELLS CAUSED A GREAT
IN SERRIED SPLENDOR OVER DECIDUOUS FOREST.
VER IN 1825. HER GREAT-GREAT-UNCLE ENGLAND,
LOR OF KNIGHTS OF PYTHIAS OF WV, 32ND DEGREE
LOWS, KIWANIS CLUB, BPO ELKS, LOYAL ORDER OF
A PEAK AT THE BARBECUE PIT AND CIDER JUG. MRS.
KINS IN A BRIEF HAND-TO-HAND ENCOUNTER. THIRD
LESNAKE, CURLED AMONG THE SOFT TINY BLUETS.
NG SUFFERING PUBLIC WILL CHORUS A LUSTY, AMEN.
NDITIONS IN MORGANTOWN. THE SOUTHERN MINER,
N CONVERSATION, TENACIOUSLY HOLDING TO THE
AY AND ONLY STOUT HEARTS ENDURED. VERILY THE
PUREBRED BEEF CATTLE. MONTANI SEMPER LIBERI.

SAW FIT

Gitmo in legal twilight, red and green hazard
     net the sea
scape beyond enduring
freedom, the nightly movie. Montage of flag,
soldier, airplane. Get more for your
money with American
express more blood from your nipples give her
more gas the Cuban answers. Our new targets
in this big hot war give more
in the presence of such women.

She is mother of all 'persons
in my higher chain' England the moon-
     face of the 72-point   matrix
of stress and duress. From wonderbread Fort Ash-
by her people raised her up, poor short-shackled to a
trailer behind the saloon and sheep-farm,
  images of a collapsed pyramid
of accountability and desire on the enamelled tiles
in the college hallway, her proud railway daddy   Detention
is an enabler for interrogation   Shut up   Get some booth time
screen door to catch the skeeters   'very, very sorry,
we are not home'   they are
tacked to wire netting.   Terrie
believes her daughter was at heart   Thinking in the dirt
Maybe England would get more from the MPs.
The gloves came off
for a new entry
whose order had been cut above.

She she wanted to be a storm-chaser, had to be dragged inside
after a tornado broadcast. A member of Future Farmers of
America, yes to Frankfort high in combats, hooked on X files.
Her best friend Destiny Goin talk to her, didn't see how their
future lay with loving parents the long fall afternoons shoot
turkey and squirrels, she declined to shoot deer theirs were work-
ing dogs, German shepherds summer came back, worked nights
at the chicken-processing plant their beaks had already been cut
off their pictures were posted on walls of honor at the courthouse
in Keyser and the Wal-Mart in LaVale. Guarantors of arous-
al, she I guess you'd call her The whip-kitten who lets us watch.

For that vast of night that they may work
the signs the gun, thumbs up, cigs, she plays cock tease
to men modelling themselves on the Rock.
In Mineral County they played from the baseline, over the
bra, under the bra, down the pants, hard
fingers gitmo operational procedures as the given
baseline for enduring   Squatting and hooded,
lactic acid pouring through thighs   cramps, side-stitches
that shall pen thy breath up

without a name or a number could any of them exist
bloats in bags of ice outside skin
and bits of flesh raining through the air.   Leasher Girl
looks a little befuddled in this one 'It was kind
of weird', she says again

The father was 'not the person who left
Union Town', who jumped out of the laundry
room, dragged his wife in her quilt to the top of the stairs,
secreted video cameras around the split-
level. A true crash edit
razor back of the trades   solidarity on a knife-edge
As for England, 'she wouldn't even drag a dog
on a lead   let alone a human' until a Titan consultant told her to

cut to the
chase

The Swift-to-Harry:
'Our challenge is to give analysts
guidance on how to extract
the most appropriate information,
as well as the tools and technologies
to reason from this data.'

'kind of weird'   speaks the voice of westerns
reason   softly   can you imagine the noises and sweet airs
the thousand twangling instruments hum sometimes voices
riches ready to drop upon me   sound beamed back
for teases in prime   get more get out of it
if not what will be the spring of your pity   crying to dream again

Geneva told us to   mind games
bopping the hooded ones with a Nerf football
but Gonzales had declared nine eleven
'renders quaint some of Geneva's provisions'
                                        the hardest to break were
flown on private-hire jets to states   famous for their facilities
                                        they called it
in the air   'rendering'   the raw thrown into an auger-grinder
batch-cooked in the chef   skimmed   sold off as an enhancer
silent partners in our food chain
                    'We thought it looked funny', she said   again

A hundred degrees in the shadows, rain of mortar
hanging out with her buds across the yard
theirs were transitory technical networks but persistent social networks
the new targets   underlings left to sweat the details
the vast of night   lit by a chemical light   fluid spilled on the ground
saying it was a knife   ghost detainees
                                'forced to crawl through it and then
placed in a dark cell, this
would freak them out because they would glow'

60

And so to England's greatest disgrace
assault consummated by battery
    'This one's getting hard'   once again, thanks technology
force tactics known as 'The Vietnam' into the media
via glare of the chemical light   shit-smeared path at least
these ones were resisting   cocked in their mouths
                                    vanitas and death's
giving head in the digital snap
shot   a year's detention   enables you to drop it
forget it   the speculum which opens the rotted
wound to congress inspectors   inside the body,
which is forced to get up off the table and keep walking

parts   not taken to the cleaners   with her lovers
taken to Bragg for abuse
of alcohol and sexual abandon   her own
performance for her boys with a multitude of different
stressed out by a tiger team   Madonna of the spectacle
Shit-boy watches through a pair of her smalls
the CO gives them England's Victoria's Secret
catalogues   to loosen them up   skeletal ladies
her lewd face in the Lynch mirror   the rough side her mouth opens
again England has no high intelligence   value   She cannot say
'I am a survivor' oop oop   she'll make her money back
get more out of the birth   above her, men, hooded
leave no paper   trail through the wreckage.

PRESENTING

SIGHT UNSEEN

Bulk and rubble forest the street,
old tiles suture together maps
of the milk trade in Delft.
Under glass the person has no name
for pre-histories of uses in the place
she began in heaving, in her house.

The lift has no colour, certainly no variety.
An arc of extremism sweeps
on spiced air, calls on the future
as a mode of transport. Her plan
for levitation still unfinished,
she is not there yet. Later

still some striving,
to rumble the country hideaway where
mowing is a big romantic alternative
and all the flesh tones live again in chipped paper.
Now broken. Now written with scores.

Between the past with its feeling for preservation
and a future practiced in a corner,
lifted on a tablet she tries to recall.
What relief ventilation can give,
what she thinks of the wind snapped
from other departments, over the trains
the adult street full of unrecyclable bulk,
when was unbreakable in trees
that saddled it
that shook it
even now to a yoke filling with wildest pathos

The future claws into sight. Gets the all clear.

Past motioning of a praying
mantis or common green fly
on the motherboard, what does it look like
from up there, the sliproad
into deep space – an irrelevance? A motion
carried in all its particulars,
the hungry scallop shell of the pelvis,
the narrow-boned paddles shape
the antique hourglass accordingly,
the narrow bone that echoes like a radio broadcast
of wrack, the builders, the drowning...

Down with flecks of brown
blood the overcompensating fist, hammering
a history on the heritage anvil. What rose
seems stubbornly inadequate – parkland,
some chases there – but still so loved
it is forever helpful, forever dangerous.

IN ALBUM MEN

I interpret, sip, clapping round the stove.
The feast this minting winter is a tube of meat.
It boils slow, the grid will not go
damp, nor the gas spit and threaten pipes with blanks
of wet air. On my wrist is a hand
it cuts both ways: all same none all same
snow leopard's evasive habits. Between them
ramping sweet
water coils down pole
cuts, and to rattling Highbury comes
slave to memory dragging chalked feet.
The present is not refundable,
in a jello mould a dead man's switch.

This is where my mind is: after the itch,
sketched in chalk and lemon thyme, near unbelievable
burrows for strangers in high rock. Past making
whites feel fresh. Buds pressed to tea,
or by the switching tongues of nervy birds
shared for a tiny lira packet of poetic staple.
This route up is quick, the dry below. Half way
to Uçhisar down in the wind, scratched, stealing
gross sexual delights from natural cloisters,
come over all
refreshed, mouth pinned with nectarine
in a forest of grotesque pillars.
By tufted peaks slots like the mail chute
pigeons to excorporate. Who mounted them
to furrow rank muck from behind
while the saints watched in half ochre
you have your answer.

I am a passing zero. Lungs cut lengthwise open
reveal an index of haste, faith, charity
bounding over terra nullius to the chapels

as they recede into the past.
In the panorama, through ears of rock
and runs to water around the cenotaphs,
through damaged red layers and green ones,
no place to stick the finger I use now
to prod the Michelin face of anglicised 'winter'.

Dispersed by bus by plane to towns
past foiling, grim fleets of crowded nights,
natured earth relaxing off road not bothered
to rise to the occasion of presence where
wild strippers fall on the beaches.
No more hope from the wind, carried by dawn
Eudemos buried ship, life short as a day, a broken wave
Mevsimlik sailors cut the Eurovision frigate in to hove
the tomb smiling for all the world like
above the gash souls climb out to fraternize.
Among the huts, the legacy applies
for its destiny on the stoop
the cash caravan sails west
into eternal kayaking. Zing
our ankles, faces distended like Yorkshire
puddings by midday, the track passes
along the aqueduct above the burials
half manic with atmosphere.
Unable to husband
this history apart from a 35mm spread
and back on show, all go swimming, giving up
imported care to the salt load.

What gives you that impression
loosened in sinus what did you see
see what there, and with what.
When you are old and purple and full of
exomine how happy were you, skull raided with
desires filled to the salt rim and tapping ochre.
Unravelling past parodies
rumbled into sand, or sketchy

like those rooting towards the water of life
flavours infusing in hot glass. Though
steep is the price, this is the methodical happiness
of earning power, strait
it is also, in all honesty left ajar.
Where do you find your land of cocaine pure entice
flattened to the tube wall with the meat bun
now you are here, wanting, speechless
as you lean towards a gap jammed with frosty cardboard.
How will this past continuing not as fixture
give back to victorian plunder, but a live
ticking the seconds and the damp regulate air.

THE COAL-SEARCHER

Arrayed on nurse's breasts with watch-pins stand the sympathies of the material world, attentive, reviewing the list of needs. The bug set in Basque oak killed off the last natural sign of the oath, pledged by men to their community. So a boy moaning under a shin of bark, his mother cruel as a chain pull   no way to get in or out of love   dies also

and with him goes all hope of enthralling the land with what is called 'native spirit'. Up in smoke and ash the moon tramps like a quarter-horse, all the trunks are quartered, knotted fibres crackle under the stress of feet. At the centre, in cinders, an act of language that set all to blazes; its mandate expired the constitutional crisis of a king with his tongue cut.

Over stunt pastures eyes narrow, looking past stump jungle gyms, searching for the identifying scar. Could the scarred field some evidence that love, compacted and ready to explode, might be somewhere to be seen, or that the ticking in its works where the water drips and the spindles smoky with speed could run along the cord to the boy in the burlap bag and detonate in his face, I would go back

home a happier person, not shudder to feed each chunk singly into the stove. But the head is hidden in a heap of slag, air consumed by hulks neither foreign nor really that interested.

CHORALE

Around the pole blooms surrogate fire. Beyond the immediate consequences sink through the stainless universal plug, as pennants for this tiny irrecoverable holiday are passed from hand to dyed hand. A grove of panels inlaid and lacquered are hinged in copper beech bark. They fold here and snap closed at the latches. Sunset, shutter round any day, the confused victim of the city: little teenage day gone out for breakfast, on Old Street with her broken neck.

Staring up through mallow through rust, past the baths of the Roman and other empires, touch some last honey with your eye. But is it honey the hope of peace entailed to all newborn; is the trench coat hung like a spod empty with no one watching, no one driving it by. Or does that hope melt and fizz like ice dropped on soda. To say nothing about the looting, spleens in blankets, the online community sleeps dug in snowcaves. For terror is the entailment. If this is the final instalment you can pick your options like rings from your fingers, stiff and bells, your neck griddled by light

folds the past in to gruel with metal markers. The little flags can be rehoused in golf courses, or the sites chosen by sniffer dogs in the garden of the children's home. But that depends on you being here, when in fact you are nowhere but a prose accomplice. Everything in a skip, cup, slate, down to the spool of a gene can be read by someone, in China. Who knows what they'll do at sun up, the scarlet flickering along the runner which marks the middle ground of the hoe-down. We won't know where to put our hands to the hammers, how to prepare the pinnace for the hot fat seas of ruin. We should draw up a plan with these tongs, sticky with the fleshes, but as hope floats we are too busy. Too busy watching.

STILL HANGING ON CLINTON'S SECOND VISIT

Hope for running out on the flats, under
the overpass that chutes this abstract
into bread home delivery, buckled up
from your front porch to my front seat.

The hyphenated bridge lane where motor
boards a dream of expansive happiness,
dinosaurs trapped in oil pits, a future
to run into red and green eyes

and out till no man's land. Past the refinery
into outlaw verde, unowned hydrotropic
life unclinched by regularity, ownership,
by a loss that has never happened: one of the

kinds of possible losses. You sang this
national anthem, your life parenthesized
by flight into cinema and depiction:
the sun sets orangely, tempers cool

the boss goes nowhere and the land,
lived from, bossily patriotic. Your name
retrieved from the web, the collocation
with the smash given to know

the unknown, blood furls gradually
from the heads and is never less
parenthetical. Texts still bundled
in your pocket switch to discreet mode, rings

engage the natural world in decoration.
Above the concrete marshes, the stars
can't make their empty lines believable.

Stars to shadow by, chase out of manhattan

where that marsh is brown and the old worlds
creep around on stilts with eeling baskets.
Banality will never be obsolete, like the internal
combustion engine: even the tracks

of unbroken yellow too fleet for
the escape artist, a mimic pile-up loops
in place of persons, in a question of sovereignty.
No place unmandated, no stretch without

the service stations marked in bold on the route planner.
These four lanes a horn of plenty blow out at night
the endless hunting lament, a fictional
surplus for continents learning to recognise their bounds.

In the outlaw west the wedding party tips
their guns into starlight glasses, fill space
with pellets to celebrate the belly's axle; fire
falling down burns a noose free, ash and sand

to put fires out and secure a slipless exit. Was this
really what you wanted, to splurge on a rider
the whole real an advert break? Do go on so,
then breath undeterred in the breakbeat meter,

singing for freedom to misuse national space:
the free ride which is no freedom
when at the edge of disaster
you find yourself in the back seat of the patrol car,

the reel catapults into pitch black, and over all of us
who still live the stars
crash down from their heroic outlines
into vacancy

SCRAMBLED

Bolded on the wall
        too big next to a spool table
flash landscape illegible
sunshine moves in
        cypher
        her legs tucked together
calling for her – for her dolly.

Hectic movement among palms
and privets
        some mammals in there
            a comb of haiku
brushing them down for.
                So a man had been

hung up here making a pyramid of light
chains in the small town evening.
        The dealer can't make any promises
        tax free or wrapped in plastic
the cup-holder and the coin-holder vying
for the extract, still warm and bluish.

The whole party shines with streakless gloss
The top of his head
        is covered by a thick wad of hair.
So a man had been
        Citing a greater, and therefore less necessary
risk.
        A horn is delivered.
Solo it sings in the presidential dawn.
Its cup covered it spits rag.
        The cocktail party   he gave up his
head when he came for the money,
traded his connections for pleasure

lost the plot simulcast the birth the election
and everyone in the piazza was like

what do you know   a wise guy
remanded to speech acts
                brief monosyllabic natural consensual
                and in contempt of   and in contempt

and when the message arrives it's just plain
scrambled.

WINTER QUARTERS

1.

Drawn out, and hung over. Ten little
cages, 91 cm^3 cozened to the wall
communal space spied on by a hole
by which money comes down
pissing it down. Upstairs
in rose light the real
ales drawn, veins to the tap,
context of another conversation about rigging
and the beyond complicity.
Net gains forgotten
a spider scores a bottom line
a pin scores your bottom lip.

Tweeze back the rind
from the intestinal war you
find a speaking toad. 'Nobility.'
Our restrictions
gabble a little cough. Below stairs
cages are empty historical curiosities.
All restraint is lateral: text moves.
Nothing is happening in forests, the cauldron of fire
is what it is, catches whisper
the oncoming straight along the rail.

2.

Freedom levitates over the green
and eyes are sealed shut with starch.
And ears in underwear, in sealing wax.
If suspected of fraud
such movements can be followed,
recognised as human from

initiation to declaration to the elaborate cut
the muscle to life the pelts.
Our new challenge of authentication. From chip
and pin presents validated
the counter cannot see
your hope for romance, your webbed feet.

COMMERCIAL IN CONFIDENCE

Our glow is tested against all greys.
A folder of air follows me home: enclosed
the overlay of pantone red, negative green
of thought
                    nightslips sometimes
around the comb-toothed manners
into rejection: seeing a fat man in your place,
a stranger more desirable than pretty knowns,
my double spines.

                    We manage also
warp mechanically levelled strips
moving our manufacture to their end-users
keeping tabs on the beautiful.
It is a way of getting by.

If the manifest says 'dejection', under the sawdust
the real cargo is full
of notes transposed to pleasure. You feel
like yourself but in joyful progression,
attain an unknown competence
wrapped on air and bone.

Big blowers of confident reality
score the sky by plan into fiscal strips.
Because you are righteous you open your
head every day, joy cut-in like a kite mark.

PARADISE GARDENS 1 AND 2

If you line up the Paradise Gardens side by side one by
one the smell of burnt sesame and broken fortune
cookies carries an entire demography out to sea.

Pink lights of frozen produce, steam trains sleeping
like a working watch can't be quiet a sand-trimmed
figure and the idle lullaby of the pet telephone.

This is where the animal spends all day.
This is the habitat of a parching corpus luteum,
the spring head of all its fabled diversity.

Whose beauty is postponed age, the unfinished
matter blowing around a gold star. Makes the outline clear. You are
beautiful, restive, you stir the air now vacant

with your achievements you will soon be
rewarded with a gingerbread monkey. Will you
please shove off? Timing heaven three stops down,

the patient earning forgiveness has accepted
a future perfect to ornament
her decal life. Up the ante, fill the circle completely charming

with a no. 2. You may get lucky. Name your poison
honestly and you could rise above Coventry
in a slipper of hosannas. I surrender to your aimlessness

costumed as self-love, because I just miss your goodness,
and no better. Flock of friendly parables catch
the air like whiffle balls. Hard to loft, they are harder to gather.

SPOKEN WORD

A.

Go to bed without supper for that
tirade about the something politician
the man in the eye-patch
overstepped viewers' tolerance for

bad language and non sequiturs. His sewer
mouth the first tip-off to the bad habits
his hands kept. At least keep them
talking till we fix the source file,

maybe get your supper yourself. Thanks
to our quick response
time not a word was lost, an input wasted.
You dream in adhesive,

dress the part in foil in apple mantle.
The set of all symbolic characters translates
into infantile graphemes your warrant
for endless and exuberant kindness.

Above the fold – the rescue chopper –
it was blooming, all white carnelian,
at one point this year the fragrant
air made itself an imperative:

to be born, not to lisp or squander
the magic premises, to crate up the
joyful tendencies in fictive constancy.

B.

But always criminal intent
punches through the stud wall
gently, like an 'anybody home'
traded by mounted policemen. Pick

through leaves looking for
seeds which might make us sick
or little animals evaded the jet spray.
Kiss his dark patch of neck

the lizard pattern of a birth
that was almost boring
you lay him down. You spend the night
hungry, gob full of statistics.

Until night falls apart poked with bird
ardour, point by point it is dotted
into bright work and wakes up

pierced by incredible speech

C.

The source is a call-box in the diamond district,
a former reporter sleeping rough. That was
an elegant speech you gave, they were full
but they really ate it up.

EXPORT ZONE

Showing the slit across the thigh, she anchors
the erotic by which burundi girls buy un
hcr relief. Is that enough milk
foaming venus blood shot through narrow arteries
sewn up with grass and thorn. Exotic
                imports unsold sweating
bushmeat, a race for extinction won at the starting
gun. Every tactic is neurotic, down to the wire

down to the long nail. Before the noon bulletin
I've sucked off two enemies and crossed
my arms over my mouth demand for
beauty on the bell curve, ringing
                the change is slight on a five pound note.

And the sign for *abcde* is camp
catastrophics, the cash transfer from london
lite to salt lick has some chick as its
sole beneficiary. Would I like her
whipped or salted
the critical assessments are in
the latest colour, mocha grande.

I sat in front of the terminal bowed by
happy news. He's coming, down the basra
                highway the eastern mainline toppling regime
intimacy fabricated across brand loyalty makes
the sky whipped to spreadable cloud, how long

to the end of sacrifice, how to hold breaths and forbear
relief until just then. The privilege of
purchase on one life, no matching gifts programme
can convince the easter season opens
                laying out purple and pink under bowed branches.

Doctors refuse to look at a local sample, even these
lines sucked tight as zippers betray
their sex with pink flapping. How to feel
pleasure when writing is a work of repressive
sympathy, how do you celebrate time?

THE KEY IS

Jesus' blood covers me, says the dandled air
freshener. Sacrifice of the undocumented
worker in the collapsing tower
Who benefits. Who is encumbered. And
laid out by a multitude of hosts, unblinking
rests between the temple and the slug
ask who benefits. Who the benefit cheats
the star of the light
ceremony impounding Harrow's
rest time is 'a very unpleasant guy', a sofa cruiser,
indeed he knows a little less about himself than other men,
the school kid nicked by a rider among them.

Frosting blackens on a ring donut.
Above new river precinct the waiting
lists away from the centre where they apply
for help, slime
on rock,
a lost child commemorated on active packaging.
Sacrifices noted on clubland vouchers
What can any of these kids want from me
I am their teacher and their nothing
giving in the spirit of an oxidised polymer.

The 'rhythm of life'
is a big distraction,
this is a drink of water.
He lives in a painted study.
In a panelled library
with carousel. In the arcade,
snuff tokens.
In buses greased with tiredness,
and in the head
of the old woman, chilled by frost.

The key is a relic, museum-piece of
alienated labour and laureate disease.
When we are hated then we are bound
to roll in hatred's rich burnt sauces,
those little sacrifices that all mothers make.
Lights go on with a bang. Heads up
and down again, driving through rain, *come*
paying members of the infest, we're counting you.

PRECINCT

I wake up hopeful
I haven't hurt anyone in my sleep
I'm back in tracksuit, tapping on the concrete
pyramid in the roundabout, held up on a stick
to a feeder lane efficiently
moved that is also a kind
of land management.

Road rings furniture stores moving little
sitting rooms along towards another southern state
claimed by chicken peddlers, spaces rushed
like bubbles in cola, locked but rentable,
or opportunity tiles and knock-down kitchens
might be knocked about or fixed. From here
grassland is intolerable. Any chaos of sand
too reductivist for formal planning
leaves mind no way to orient, makes
a brain turned to defrost
or to jump (like me in airs) from link
to consequenceless link, weep patent nokia.

This day is young; innocence will soon come
in biodegradable bottles. Out past
the potted meat, cleaners and a church
kept deductible by some foreign blacks I read
there is a garden stretching to great lakes, on top
a mountain browed with ice beetles.
There birds intend to be ladies
pearls in their tears are wireless hotspots.
So it tells us when it turns up with an energy
drink and a faceful of unfiled dreams;
light, foam, up at two then suddenly...

That's when the words come full of fang and wind.
Perched on a Juliet-balcony, looking backwards

out of a maisonette towards the smoking circular,
where do the words fly – like the kisses, pilgrims,
where. Into a zone derelict of all restraint,
a city aerated by military-adept caterpillars
– that's another formal plan to move energy
along, turn over rock and home
in on land-management. There set down in rings
of fat and wire that trim the heads
of boys fed on grass, somewhere else
that may never yet existed.

ERGON

Work from home encased in plastic. Is it
born or learned gentleness, can
ungreased applications be worked in
no sweating   Work for
cardiac health, go past dinner for broke
go throat backed up with morals
not to do anything different but keep
go   And backed against the lists
scare easily.

The jenny has slowed to a piano
echo of jets uncurling
landing gear, sliding into slowness.
There is always travel to punctuate
the repetitions of control s, of text
manufacture. To ride out all day, into the emptiness
that randomizes commercial premises,
to open the anatomical right at its hinges
then swing into free space for family life…
Where routers feed contamination right up to the wall.
Heels are hard and white/
in white hands the multi consistencies
hang about, like a wave snagged in a pin.

A fear of home not working, work that
makes time slide
through oils liquidising a window,
is a hook for the exterior.
Drawn outside – that space
for exploring what doubt is, what's
too much saturates the fear of arrest
equals fear of being moved too far.
These forces stabilise the skeletal building
breathing in its jacket, ears bathed in female
garage cycles, faking the passion to hoot.

Light little candles stuck to postcards
or prepare for colour supplements
E-numbers that shake
the brain's soaking lentils
depend on discrimination, and make it.
Live feed can disrupt the chain of administered logic
or idleness wrap the head cleaner with fluff.
Meat distracted with adrenal awareness,
how it comes to an end in a squeeze-box.

But how about the fear of working,
like a tramp needs a shave from a strap, a retreat
from time beaten through shameful picnics
in tv studios? Ahead could be flattened
and thick, carried away in bits by ants,
whose apparatus belongs to no one and trips
unclad into clover. So that was you hnh,
paralysed and hunted in the sidestreets, overturning
trusts. You are an animal again,
unable to control your own increase,
sugar levels limited day and night.

When can we meet in the space mall. It is stupid
not to be able to name your supplier
in the class action of work to life we split;
as sure as I sit here I have no trouble
considering that, it is my job
to be randomly analytic.
That you wear my white hands like a twin.
In the garage calypso echoes neither joy or
sorrow but the simple fact of repetition.
Choices purged by the limits
of space, air
miles the rewards of travel. Another half billion bodies
have just been declared obese. How much
easier to believe as I tuck in that little remnant of tail
that you alone are hurtful, crippled by your extreme
hatred of the whole structure of organised labour?

THE DAY RATE

1.

The news didn't relieve us, potentially
drawing along a notch in a hot-pink stick
what was folded in hot batter the other week.
Hours got lighter by exhaust and prevented stain.
We think, we can grow our company. Cupboards
stuffed with nuts and dates, radix angelicae
safflower and weakened water, shampoo

of egg yolk, sinless blanching toothpaste: to be ready
and always good enough, clean for quickening.
We didn't use to be religious. But the round head…
My hands began to bloom, and my feet in shoes,
even with blood thinning up the elevator shaft
and further work for the taxable heart I arranged
the weeks for my hall monitor. Sighted.

2.

Awake in a topography of this new gut, which I
bisect and tap for waiting echo:
thins over the tape, tugs the ring-pulls on each corner,
or solaces a disruptive kid in carbonated
but is never known to gripe in the cellar.
We took a little hope from such good conduct;
in isolation wards the sound would be muffled alien.

But when change ends hope ends of a different life.
We have managed to get this far without water,
but the vehicle slows and stops in the middle of nowhere
tires overblown like cartoon puffs, macadam broken.
After rushing wind the silence is like nothing,
but after all it is not actually quiet, the blades and beads
push vocally from the ground and you all continue.

In everything you make by that continuing
I will register and sit back down, and the air will fall on me.

3.

Ready now call in the evac unit. Transitions from promise
to fiduciary agreements are never easy, but we try
to make things simple, drawbridge over
the Great Dismal Swamp guarded by experts
in flushing out insurgency. My arm buzzes

as the intruder creeps into the citadel,
then I am half-awake in recovery, and light as plastic.
I will be able to run again, a literary agent
interring the future pattern when it drops again;
the light is wakeful, not quiet, the front again calm
but those will be some days until I can believe
anything I read without feeling singularly human.

THE GLOUCESTER, THE ILLUSTRIOUS

20-31 July 2006

Job: 'Am I a sea, or a whale, that thou settest a watch over me?'
God: 'Canst thou draw out leviathan with an hook? or his tongue
with a cord which thou lettest down? He maketh the sea like a pot
of ointment.'

Some spill onto Trenton, take the Med waters
flat up to shelves of brined rock
and holes which housed the Cesnola collection.
Behind them the chimera bursts
suddenly into gas, air, and wind of the desperate.
Felched from the wound jam tarts
chicken sandwiches, by etude struck up
the quartet in full-concert dress,
peace sweeps a 70° arc with ultrasound humane repellent
straight into the plastic rind of the oxygen mask. I can
stay here, incorporating the silence with Sudoku lettrism,
gyroscope trained on the birth gimbal of a new middle east.

The gentleman from Peachtree City
and toddlers in strollers slip the whirlpool
cliffs of recently refurbished holiday flats.
Treated to an ice-cream on the Iwo Jima they get
some freshened air. No one needs to
retreat the meadowed clips of abandoned cities,
much less die trying in a GPS mosaic, a pun
for Saigon or New Orleans drifting so white and ready
to celebrate the advances in strategic bombardment
from Sarajevo to scorched fells of cedars.
Much less *him*, and some in fact are weeping
as the embassy extracts them, siphons them
directly into the duty-free enclave.
'We were expecting to have to row boats to Cyprus,
so this is amazing,' joked Nawal Zahzah, 16, of Long Beach.
Though the tonic is flat, Mars sweet if sticky,

any taste in the white of an egg,
it's still an *out* through the windows
on liberty crushed temporarily in their casements
by cruisers pawing the flattened. The resistless air.

Out into the fields of ozone where the ancient
cannot survive without conditioning
who have wisdom with them, tasting their blue
meat, cookies, and national guard protection in Saint
Louis and LA, now that universal logic has stripped from it
the benzophenone which separated our days
          passed away as swift ships
from the leadership vacuum
paraded by black space. Let the Marines reverse to their proving
the ambassadorial franchise where they were once served.
'It's like going to see the Colosseum in Rome' said Lance
Cpl. Nicholas Miniard, 21, of Cincinnati,
or the amphitheatre at Albanum where Acilius
killed the lion himself to entertain an emperor.
Helping Americans get on board
an idea floated by the Germans, seas' fire
who assay the values at the foundation
of our relationship with Israel
measured by Qana in twice metric tons.

Out on the Orient Queen this Thursday, starring
prawns on ice in the gourmet restaurant,
Lindsey Lohan – star of the sea – learns
to be fat on gloss. And for the children,
Harry Potter and the Goblet of Fire
manages the terror of the flat screen.
An odyssey of 12 hours to Limassol whose flow
green lights and tongue-tazers manages from the table
in a rainbow room with Rice, Annan and Solana.

Aboard the Bulwark, or maximising
the steerage capacity of Illustrious and Gloucester
'there's a real buzz' 'when you look at the faces you feel'

the shock of corn coming to its grave in full age.
White handkerchiefs on the Naqora cliffs wave them off,
the pride of the fleet,
too fast to take anything but
one piece of hand
now steamer trunks melt down their elements:
leaving the same ironic radiant dust,
the same necrotic powders,
the same patient sleepy clusters.

As the sparks fly upward, so do benefits in Bethesda
for those first in after the troubling of waters.
The dogs of war crash at their hotel, watching animal
related movies and licking lactose-free ice cream
from syndicated saucers, finding
Nemo in orgasmic eternal loop. Cats awake to fifteen minutes
of stroking, alive to the world through their reception
of care on the underside of paid hands. The price
does its part for the $40 billion America spent on its pets,
who spend their days in wealth
and in a moment go down on contract.

In the bomb shelter the bride crouches
beneath a blue huppa to pledge her determination,
breasts full of milk, bones moistened with marrow,
though Home Front Command instructions
do not permit weddings within the range of Katyusha rockets.
The hasbara effort is a machine well-oiled
by years of combat training and dumb spit,
Ariel Sharon is squeezed
in an iron lung until he belches out his resilience
a body poured out like milk, curdled like cheese
and pasteurized under heavy superior heat.
During this time of crisis, follow us live on your cellphone,
bluetooth the kids in Sidon
'black as shoes'. Or wait for a text from the IDF:
time for Ibrahim Mahmoud to abandon his houses. Whistling
overhead comes a shark of metal with pain in his teeth

for any children you might not yet have roused.
Far from safety, they are crushed in the gate,
neither is there any to deliver them by
Atlas Air via Prestwick and Mildenhall
but Jesus nuts are engineered locally,
Redmayne gives us fire
and forget capability
not to be blank or lazy, remembering our brief happiness
as a million flaneurs marching Pall Mall.

'We're dealing with two faces of this tragedy,' said the mayor of
                                                    Bhamdoun.
'The sad situation of the refugees and the fleeing tourists.'
For those feeling the heat, the Bekaa Valley has no traffic.
Stress can cause chest pressure, feeling
short of breath, arteries hard as the nether millstone,
loss of appetite for empathy. Who esteems
iron as straw, brass as rotten paper.
You need to get away.

By night: the devil of mid-day spreads panic
and destruction wasting at noonday,
as thermographic images on the heads-up display
and the pre-emptive technology of the new Volvo
forecast higher temperatures and a little rain

> *of milke and blood, when M. Acilius and C. Porcius were
> Consuls, and many times els besides it rained flesh: and looke what
> of it the foules of the aire caught not up nor carried away, it never
> putrified, yron in the Lucanes countrey, the yeere before that M.
> Crassus was slaine by the Parthians, and togither with him all the
> Lucanes his souldiers, of whome there were many in his armie.
> That which came downe in this raine, resembled in some sort
> Sponges: and the Wisards and Soothsayers being sought unto, gave
> warning to take heed of wounds from above.* (After the
> fighting, the Syrian spoils were found in Glabrio's own
> house, while Cato the Censor repaired the aqueducts,
> taxed adornment and campaigned to destroy Carthage.)

Listen to the mandolin rain, listen to the music on the lake
Listen to my heart break every time she runs away
in summer rain, stumps swapping the grass,
soft waters washing down the strips and Sheba'a farms,
aquifers bursting with song, with figs and lighteners,
adventure sports and rafting on the Litani.
'It was like rain: we got wet, they got wetter'
poeticized Col. Ofek Bukhris in Bint Jbeil
robotic in the shade. And Bush? His roots are wrapped
about the heap, and seeth the place of stones.

CULTURAL AFFAIRS IN BOSTON

She Cannot Take Any Credit For This One.

Slingshot from the rust belt
comped to the commonwealth,
keep your eye out for the mass spikes
puritan sign: the horizon gets uppity, folk
                picking on their porches in the dashboard
                picking sacred harps in cartoon cloudland –
we're getting religion as endless corduroy
bends upward into blue hills. What kind of relics
will we be,   toxic twinkies
                        haughty french dressing
please end on a high note, and let our spoils
full pay with interest on the departmental i.o.u.

Pilgrims spill out of the suburban,
the regular army training in sculls
points us up the Charles towards Winthrop
and guacamole from Grendel's kitchen,
Robin tears his Reuben limb from limb.
                By the sword we seek peace, but peace
                only under liberty. 85¢
tokens for the T; that is the same 7-
eleven, same shoes, adulthood
                condensed by rackrents
keeping warm the original settlement
like a fur fringe to a sad perturbation.
                These hauls are ok
                you can get warmer, thanks
to Bouchard's booklist starting at the beacon,
make our way across the common.
If the Ghost of Joy Street could tell
us where to locate
                        cheap sex, oysters, beanfeasts,
Pusey and Lamont have nothing on him

or the boys who washed their clothes in buffalo.

Offload the surplus at barker is mounted
the double veritas shield our sideline,
a final diminishable triplet makes good
as they can under the eyes of John Harvard.
We do to gog as we've done to roam,
a staged reading as the pretribulational event
afterwards it's hoped for a kind of rapture:
may the poets be hung on hooks
as catchy as the cola-mark turned to Love,
and this is how you speak to me now,
are you some kind of invading army?
Speaking to Sam and Dan, Nancy and David,
Michael and Michael and Teddy Roosevelt
and Percy Lowell, to the engraved Emerson
Bulfinch and Agassiz, to all of you and Chronos
billeted in the corner, bred from chaos to Rambo-
sinewed adulthood, his jersey
over his face like a blinded goal-scorer;
and to the inflatable clock keeping modernity
in check. The storm of debris lashing
the single-glazing, we retire to grafton
to deflate the speech-balloon,
kill the lights and unclip the roving
mike from disney wings.

Now bring forth the beast that ruled the world with's beck,
And tear his flesh and set your feet on's neck;
And make his filthy den so desolate,
To th' 'stonishment of all that knew his state.
Youtube ornithocheirus crumbles
by a water-source after his dumb mating dance,
took thermals to cross the ocean and set up
shack here with his condemned flock. So
I'm told by the little genius. Pups scramble around
bouncing Hazel, and the migrating
are their descendants or everybody's.

Making way for legal seafood, damp taleggio
and this Dialogue between England Old and New.
Joy street intaglio,
faust ink hot on an infinite switch
hidden in potential until screwed to the paper.

FRIENDSHIP I

The bride wore a Moroccan hood.
One of us tumbled through her crinoline into nettles,
or streaked the blue Latin vaults bare-chested.
Between the places at table, so many
facts were known, and the links colour-coated
fastened in on a long, slow upward grade.
Resolve, dissolve, in turn
becoming someone else. Where love was once
there is always calm, even fake calm;
and these rampant joys, collateral
with which I buy this time the underwater
watch it wanted: how to account for them,
to thank you all for my life?

FRIENDSHIP 2

A swan fell out of the sky on Stamford Hill
and was kept by the Medway sweepers in a box.
When you are fitting on the street
and the mobility scooters cut an eight
around you, the structure of complicity
becomes two simple layers: you're on the horizon-
tal, strangers at the wheels of the vertical
as they turn you to the best side or else leave
you in pudding where you are. Who do you know
you can call, your chest gripped with phosphates;
is the street a loose shuffle of objects,
impeding your return to the softness
at home, in a skanky bed? A body can suddenly
lose its way through them. Concrete
has a particular note for children,
we did scab it along our heads. In that flat
moment when the skeleton gives way,
with rhetoric, and the motor unplugged in your pocket,
let us come back to you with hazel
and quiet, to tilt the frame on its familiar axis.
I retain myself by knowing your names in danger.
Emerge in dayglo to me, from the world sick as paper.

FRIENDSHIP 3

We never thought that one was any good enough for:
no quote around that opening, no lie of transmission
as if we intended to save you to your face.
The socialist heart can organise its fidelities
in millimetre strips; we pay out greedily, your grace
and favour attainments, the bridge of your head. Mean
while forgetting that all our accounts are scrutinized
in the department stairwell, even ours. The cut-back
the baton-twirler of cuts back is a totally forgetful animal.
Synchronic faulters busy themselves throughout England,
the beam on which the eye vaults pure paperweight narcissus.
Until, that is, we are finally caught in the act
of introducing our own discovery, sip over, the bottom
falls out lets hesitancy flood into like lice the talkers.
Then it comes to our attention that nothing ours
like the fantastic. In that fantasy, you are wild on tablets,
lofted in spangled pants, the statue of our liberty:
we no more go to the parties, and have not protected you.

FRIENDSHIP 4

Girl in disney vibrato dresses herself crudely.
Life fills up, even with actors; the mill stone
is dressed in heavy bangles made in thailand, the house
rocks with its own material weight. She is in the middle
of it, dodging a column of air targeting
her with 14.7 lbf of pressure. You were closer
than you knew, dripping
from the fill of life as it spilled greasily over.
I don't mean to go back to all that;
but in the traumatic puppet-theatre
of the half night, a shape plays out
their familiar substitute, and that shape is...
I am confused by the time
it takes to restaff these visions. Make the present
sleep, as the kid isn't ready for bed,
calls to play. *Our* childhood
together, my half-desire for you, the proximity
of fantasy in so clear: here are eighty-eight memories
each ripped to the hard drive, leaving
a ghost image in the open window. I could count
my age in distance
from so many incidents I believed were final.
And wanted to state that the practicalities
of diminished tenderness are disorienting: you live
a past out too lividly, rim of an eye.

FRIENDSHIP 5

They were everywhere. A human chain
at the tables laid in feathered
love for them. Their troubles were delayed,
and joy for each other so overtook them
they could hardly speak to each other
in the usual language. Your schemes,
your infertility, your ruthless joke,
the tense flexing between your two
relationships: all smoothed under
the late light, the early matter. I am proud
and not faint of heart I change
my status in front of you: a word can do it.
Affinity swells into a giant dumpling!
We have never wept for each other
or broke the back of faith for advantage;
nothing is out there in the silence
but that day. The day flashes.
It looked great: it was great.

A FOLLOWING SEA

Interrupted this hero of faith turned inward during a dawn
raid of the kitchen condiments, pots filled with sweet medicines
jars with ears cupped to the tranquil surfaces.

All matter that waits, also this machine according to its
particular dynamics rising. By radio my operation
is coordinated to Ilium, rebounding tenax vigor

fills my sleeve. In the bushes a fox barks, a mouse plaints,
jays boss for their money a hunk of coconut fat
dangling from the blitzed tree.

This suburban spur is the inside, settled by curled
darlings of the law in whom the law
has bred and a family myopia: carding all night by the rules.

For little birds have white cheeks, and children singing
teacher teacher in eastern harmony are rosy like the dawn
when the tribes assemble on a double yellow.

Over the girl the orbital rises, following her car
tagged on the bangle of the road. It revolves under the wheels,
their confident play on the flat out, reaching toward blasted south.

Same geometry since the day you were born. Where they are
falling below the footprint of this house
that settles it into a curve of clay, north London

gully increases the overburden of the earth.
She stoops and waves our arms conducting
the run out to the borders of her abrupt fact – she knows

no different, poking the sudden dark of the screen, limits
appearing in the middle of that extense potence which people
make opposing her. The plurality of the earth

works the cyclamen returning
'alpine snow' potted at the step. These miniatures
and simples given me to concoct run the house over

to care with jars for the inhabitant animals,
to create continuity for my family, the clash of tambours
announces the repeated day. It is never and nowhere

different. Hours filter savage plenty, we follow the water
in which we drop the child's name,
where she can follow it down.

THE MUSEUM OF CHILDHOOD

They are hard, and peach across. Or they
flutter down into their nightly rest unharmed.
What can fear tell them how thickens the air,
unhampered by any sleep goes out barefoot, tries
mounds bristled dry around deleted uses.
Rebound into the messed up chorus, a child
sitting on or hanging from every branch, black faced
and hollering with hunger. Look around at the vents
of shired quadrangles, parking spots of a world
never on loan, always over there, and just so now,
as the switch of eye flicks open a bus window.
Go little cadet, you have no more time
and dance around the stumps and nets in grace,
even then seeing the veil come off like a vest
at the rec, fake coins flutter around the brim.
Oh how vain you are, icy with wheels and frills,
seeing yourself abounding everywhere: the swing links,
the drain, the tennis balls that scream through the air.
Nothing will snap shut, but only emptied
and fall open like a big pouch; then to write
in recompense, tag the remaining of the numbered scripts.

FANTASIA

Balloted shingle after which
distance to the poles is blue aesthetic.
Below this tin body, plunged in
water made slick by the running
of Singapore and the Princess
of Alaska, stretch some places
black juvenile tissue, steeply important
for transfixing the blunted in
route from homeland customs.

Vermiculated and cool. Made half
way to air by chipped cedar. Redder.
Not this homeland where the terrace
where tracks crackle from the lea
valley, a nut in a biscuit box,
and the interim in which someone is yielding.
Faces opened like ground meat in pastry,
but were so bold that nothing else was noticed
in the interim which slipped over fingers.

These are made with hibiscus. Now below this
tin corset, organic cotton plugs insert
meetings breaked by outlook reminder.
Settles here among flat-packed furniture
eternally picking its nose. Easy remember
discomfort, drunk with panic of waiting
to slide into that part of the itinerary,
to roll up pants in surge.

They are numberless in summer,
never repulsed, inventive, pull up
gaping at the chance
to achieve their dream. All that
softened water unseparated,
suddenness in cars and stations swoops

over shut heats, schools and inhibitions;
so bold that nothing was mortal
nothing intangible torn to floating rib
by the animal breath got up among the pigeons.
It is human breath, youth tears itself.

These owned winds, videotape
paused on madder,
rummaging in root. So balm, so chilly
driven from the hip. A set of islands
murmuring blue over the speakers indicts:
it is a cool thick message. These were
once our spaces, then our desires played
in super 8 on a pine backdrop
which *ab initio* belonged to someone else.
Since then we have let ourselves
be run through to look on
land, lap and room
get organised by state poisons,
the fantasy itself predicted:
nothing but the opposite
of their customs to declare.

We are losing our time.
But while we are still
up here in the dark flock of angels,
free in flight to stamp
our goods with their origin
– deep polar waters – be
ripe and might make it.

Further limit under rim of summer cannot be
imposed. Flow of declaration,
is saying *sink a hand in me,*
I thicken like milk as you turn me.

THE REAL AND IDEAL

Do not divorce your body from the field.

The darger draws the asphalt track up
and out of the uncut grass, away to the left.
There with an unbleached head
goes the younger girl, a peer for turning in place
drive the lightening of endless choices through her sock:
free price, free will, jogging out towards a remote end
in a secret city. All ends are remote, and not least

this day, dispersed over the map by its content.
                Flowing with energies drawn off voices
                cycled from speech given in gift and with
                perfected sense of understanding.

It seems like nothing. When you missed your calling
you were probably wrapped
in butcher's paper, warm, mixed, fatty.
So many times you have found it there

It looks outside the footprint of this house
like a magic workshop, tumbling in mechanics
and flash memory, toppling
on the verge of a language which hardly knows
it needs it. From this mist is safe deposit
as if the bulk were still erasable,
or the scholars born by exponent
would in future fail to discriminate our values.
Everyman was a pervert, they'll say,
his dog microchipped and neutered, and the users
generally agreed in theory.

But don't don't suck the air out of a bladder
and let it turn your head: beyond sea foam
or the fortunate in Star City

such empty spaces best uncontemplated.
Content kills the war of fact, people
in zoos and the million subtle relations
which emerged only into prose in the age of things.

That kid over there lacks content, and so moves.
Happiness is the end of all politics,
where the day worker comes to rest behind a film.

The film moves. It shows wings,
wings beating slow as resting hearts
magic lanterns balanced on parades of grass –
or maybe they are just hearts.
And they move. They are braced for the end.

FINE-LINE GHAZAL

Road noise waits at a skylight. Through breaks in
perpetual rain, light picks up your outline.

Business is done. The night wanders us in
to health, so the following meanings are fine.

As the true fiction in that frame is:
we assume a resting angle, not sick with wine

or drawing the thought out on trouble's bow
string, intrigued by the cut word, the broken line.

The globes can fire perpetually outward,
making the void free where they shine.

For nothing less than chance has spun them
into array, wrapped in oxides, a skinful in twine

wraps the self like a match. Who flares
and winds down alert in gold. No sign

of difference, except in the stems of the bond,
recognition prices each flutter of the spine.

This is an end of variety: to be sure,
that we are here, that your face is mine.

Now the fresh mint and chive, and the folded leaf
of parsley, and the cupid buttoned on branches
the haughty canon of the nightingale hoisted
that honeyed song I am joy in him, and joy in the lip
and joy myself, in him, my tender, my major; girdled with
all parts, with a joy invading
that wipes the floor all territory, but my boldest
is the boy, he follows all other joy.

Hush ah! like death in perplexity: in Manhattan I was lost
sighing and mapless, caught in a warren of thought,
bandits folded me in burlap, and I wind
thoughts napped in darkness. Fuck it, lovers, porters,
I'm a hackney victim, all baggy telephones and gold
crackling in a wallet, no mates, no bosses. Shouldn't you
be roughing him up for a penny, not leaving me
shoeless and broken-boned on the lone buckled street?

Marvel how I keep treading the poundmill, pocking the walls
with my groans, but never letting the oldest vowel nibble his ear.
When I see him, he blanks me, fine eyes of blue plate so
become him, the little caplet I can remember –
I'm ready to run him down, burst my sneakers and scald the pavement
with my skin. I would strip off, down to the bone tip,
if I weren't as wet as thyme and nervy: I've never clapped
on a body so close cut, so hot boxed for love's opera,
who's so slow with me, still as a lounger.

If I could only conjure, sleight the eye with my fist,
those bushes I'd magic into babies, so neither they
nor any other women and men would prick us out in a line
up of their petty wounds and insurgents, or gabble
their pitiable insults behind our backs.
Then I'd surely see my signor ruddy as a duke,
his bel'occhi, his fresh colour rise for congress:
I'd kiss him on the mouth every sense and direction,
he'd wear my kiss like a burning december.

A translation of Bernart de Ventadorn

THE PIETIST

You've surrendered your obsessions to noise.
You imply a model, or you would lead from the front.
You carry your organs in quietness.
You lie: you are a turbine of liquidation, habitually.
You have something in your ear, memory?
You had another life in pictures.
You repeat tenderness as rectitude.
You have no other viable model.
You like not viability but pleasure and an option.

Your options are strictly limited.
Your present is habitual but only temporarily.
You have an entry and an exit.
You are this size (actual photograph).
You remember burning.
You practice finger-picking.

You'll try anything once until you are finished.
You prise open the insides with great delicacy.
You have a reservation.

Your temperature can't be measured.
You work solidly for the rest of the afternoon.
You are a pump.

You approach and align your axis with love.
You tell only half your dream.
You remember the cars, the soldiers.
You feel it slipping through your fingers.
You give yourself entirely to this world.

You are wondering what to say.
You fold up their tired limbs, kiss their complex faces.
You unwind with cooking.
You have placed an order.

You think in lines, then lose them for want.
You want green fields of absolute clarity.
You are driven by postponement.
You embrace postponement as an ethics or maturity.
You are nervous at first then, growing in confidence.

You make your house a model of noise.
Your front is an entry and an exit.
You practise tenderness as pleasure.

Your rectitude is a pump of great delicacy.
You dream of giving yourself entirely away.
Your world is this size and order.

You fold postponement into green fields.
You are liquid with wanting.

You say what the spirit aligns on ledges.
Your lines are not short, not broken, not wanting.
You are driven by this contradiction.

You contain the heat of multiple desires.
You are not identical to statements.

SUNG TO SLEEP

Our country's enemies snore in the safety catch,
dream about owning everything
the neighbourhood is their accessory
they take to the air to advertise their species.
What viewer could believe them
that a locum spirit floats life through it,
connecting all in death and harmony,
that there is a god for forces: in spring
a diverse country
blots moving randomly in vacuums
everywhere full of water, and so full of life.

In a second they will open their anthers
and leave the carcass of their companies in process yellow
up to insurgent stalk. In each punch
bowl of vegetal fibre, sunk nearly to dripping
over the edge of its singularity,
the line,
what have we come to expect a little fruit
for decoration: cool, paralysed, crispy,
waste of cells going crazy on the tongue.
If anything happiness is
our common predicament, not
knowing how to live in the bulge where our lives
bottom out, unelected but popular incumbents, build capacity
to make choices from
a given list.

What gives to the raider, and to the day
blistering with tropical smells and agitations
against the double glaze to get inside a cool study;
to the patron or the slumming trader, means
tested but no uncertain exchange. As the cycle
trips back along the path paved with interest
no small wonder,

who will deny her

that happiness laces together the emulsions
skin she can't shed; that it is most like damson
liquor in the morning, runs
in trunks throughout the videophoned day

and hardens as it cools for supper. See it up there
gold lamé and orange powder
stooping to get you, tearing down the street. So happy
I would be sung to sleep by the noises. That capacity
hovers unyielding over us, whatever we take
to prevent it. It's the force of matter as extension,
and will break us, or us it.

VISION IN NEUTRALS
a coalition pastoral

Boring as the cured, satyr goes ice-
skating over hoggin: that arc breaks the wet
land like a spoon. That's no simile, this
is no paradise, the reserve bank for
sick thirst in history post
dates cholera and whooping
coughs and cranes. Damselflies
whittle and honey drains, but the sign
next to your face is not for your hand.
It's not even for your head, because it prepares
that same field. Nymphs crackle in staggy water.

Your satyr keeps out of site, a vole below
the dip line. The dipped sign recognises
no danger; even two wounds keep
aseptic, blown on by the violent
branching of cowslip is no worse
than a work flow diagram your friend told you
about like it was a story. A necklace
of antidotes – bring the boring one
over – rusts on a stile.

User bouncing in low-tops leaves
nothing for her trackers, not a bent cane
for Indian fantasy, she is all lost. Like an
interpretation. Taking care into
the precinct, bound to the shock-belt,
acts as preservative. To foil no inquiry
no act of jake aggression, not to intrude,
you fellow are sole trader in harms.

The red data book crunches like popcorn.
There goes another one, Caravaggio of relentless
slowness distributed by paving like a biscuit,

your harm repeats the domestic lesson. Pork!
Changelings who obsess with food, who sprinkle,
trail, go back, breaking off the house,
whose stick finger nails a prosthetic life
fumbling the touchscreen in the middle of its
most tender anecdote. He plays the emergency
where he gets kicked in the head by your satyr,
downsized by his aunty in the stupid edible house,
but you grebe, know bittern, even the incr
edible anger of coots everywhere, their nasty pointed heads
do nothing here there is nothing to do but play.
No air will take looking at longer, it wavers
away from yr eye-beam over the reed bed.

Here there is no place that does see you,
says the laminate, there is nothing
to confront. Sparrows gather unrepentantly, cause no
inconvenience to the city of logs. It wants
contract to be the face of coalition: neutral,
tedious, feebly hopping back from gothic
pollutes to organised generality diagrammed
by marker pen. Smooth newts levitate.
Who learns to appreciate the small species,
weighing jewel wings, never need
risk the shock of ultimate blankness
of their managed landscape.

I hold three in my hand: characterful, small,
scaffold life. In the movie I might
need to eat one to prolong the species.
Is fantasy cored by pleasure,
must bypass a metal fringe to make pleasure
achievable without pain or downsizing my ethics
myself? Who do I have to kill?

The regular trespasses onto
extreme love, and yet in that movie joy and grief
are twin frenzies and wholly free:

no receipts, no going for a glass of drink, no shoelaces
and chips for posties. Like the madman of Abydos
the neurotic wakes up from her session dead
angry, and thereafter keeps to the track
to protect the fragile where there is nothing
to fear here, nothing.

The reed bunting doesn't bite. You don't need
specialist equipment. The grass snake evaporates,
makes way for your orientation. Though the teals
are drunk they don't tease your accent, you have
no sprays. Dock gives itself up, and the water,
who would trust it. Diagrams show
this is all historic, flat and generous
as a piece of rice paper. Midges sing
of the missing satyr: no serial killer in that one,
sunshine indicts a path to better living.
This is your chosen country.
Nothing has to happen.

THREE SONNETS

1.

The fugitive impresses on his break
With ankle straps that tighten to the mouth,
And steering off by angels' vapour streaks
He guides his working data toward the south:
Where gardens wait to internalise his art
And watches over animals go mute,
A temperate mistress invoices his heart
While robots gently press his working suit.
Remaindered at my desk, I bridge the gap
Abandoned by his fiction of escape,
Resolutely hanging from the strap
Bound hand to mouth in anti-rodent tape.
The flight of the gods an antidote to choice
Between the husk of duty and the voice.

2.

Lay down your sweet life.   Stop up the sewers
that excavate the feeble neighbour,
decorate clobber. Your enemies in vans
tremble, harangued by exhaust, bulletins sour
or roses whitewash the blood-transfer unit
where human feed is patiently tabled
but you are floating on a nest of pink
invisible to film through the public park.
To live in constant joy is no good.
You must solidify for others a moment
the accident a natural fix, the highways buckle
as SO-102 approves your instant consumption:
theory blackens your name,
against hunger you are pathetically lightless.

3.

Can you recognise Daniel, his bent?
Assume this is his eye. Was it mangled
or smaller than a barrel, would the triangle
of his specifics enter just here? Does the rent
struck in half like a cat mask interfere?
Has the fold been done right. Judging by this key,
was he closer or twisted like rigging or mostly free?
It has none of his expression, I see, the smell of fear
and spit caked in his ear, Condillac with a stain.
He was taken away at six months' grace,
lived in yellow polyester on an assembly line.
Invited to identify the remains,
you see nothing in the limitless ardour of his face
to operate more specifically against your time.

REX

with Ayla ffytche

Fierce rhinos blot out the sun.

All through the fruit trees, fictive
calm lathers your radiant birds: face down
an arch of guardians, difficult to hold
the heat of cambrian teeth. Whippets
strung like lights in the branches,
do you hear that sound from the hills
is it astronauts on fire in wells.

Spiders darling
               hold the eye shut it won't close
in time all white is gloomy and sisters
               perish for their anchors
bust them to the ground.

   Speed's britain has heads on his knees.
               The ancient flies
         without wings as seed
         clapped in pink skin is pagan,
                       then the body gives in singing
                       memorial hymns to the

head bastard, wind-bag, floating along,
the deputy says 'just look
at yourself!' in the golden mirror
and that purple fiction is dead
you can see by his brown heart, his fixings.

END OF DAYS

All radical signs by which on These radical brackets all around
the component times, by which We select Good luck
beauty hard and shining like   Pearls, and Lozenges
phrasing all these renegade times into the divine message. Choose
Choose to bless. Choose to bless the day falling
into brass jack pot. *I remember all*
the days, they play before my eyes sometimes
I go to watch the ovens rich in natural vitamins
feeding off myself, my dreamed-for.

For too long, sorting tickets in the shade of the thorn
that penny drops affixed to Find
the opening palm these aces allude
to   this life, the desired, and even when dark
fills its haunches with ice and fire I have been on it,
on full voice coarse or passionated, a bundle of nerves
And each with their own head. As I go on I go
west idiotic, free to shout like nothing saffron.
I'll go to that country, the beautiful one

in the cockpit if I learn my trig. The sign says No
equivalence between those who take pride in dying
and those who vow When speech is the real action
The sign is an impress blowing down and east out,
treadmills backwards to an origin where that time
split into component sprockets Two incisors
splitting each other by their petty alignment. *If it's like this*
at the beginning what will it be like in the end The infant learns
to recognise his box by infinite difference How
he discovers his father in the line up a testament
to his faith that he is made
for recurring These times are familiar we
pluck our joys choosily from the sky before it
burns out the last branches.

in honour of Mohammed Haithem and Suleiman Mahmoud

SELF-POSSESSION

The internal hand is pale enough
it could be boneless, but for the jitters;
in the world its crimes are endless.

> Where is my mandate, shot up
> from a cordite touchpad on the edge
> of freshly manured fields, pulled down
> and tacked under protruding alien veins.

I go out and around. The lane leads
to the capital, big wave, split rocks,
an orgasmic catastrophic curve backs in
to roost in my broke-up terra cotta.

> And all I can think to say is
> thanks for that. Take a swipe. This is the hour
> for the radox accumulator, let concepts
> write themselves on universal machines.

And swings out again, is a free gift.
This is the syndrome as thought, a self
suckles on the world's fibreglass wounds.
It is not an excuse. Do you take credit?
Double the billing rate for puns and weapons,
being kind to ladies' fears? Another way

studies the curve of my baby's head for a
do-it-yourself parthenogenesis. Head-lag
is a fearful nominator.

> At least that shut it up if
> all day long you live with the shakes
> you have to keep up the food, the warmth,
> the play without video, because panic won't feed
> what needs feeding every other hour.

The hand grabs
and cups from both sides
like a cultivator.

DISPLACES

'The truly happy are clean and beautiful.' Sophist, 230e.

Dug in my opposite number, the present
need to be soluble like muscle
how patient it is, its craft enclosures
and through it: we the live-ins who stroke
home air a wet brush fine, dragged or bold
approach through shade press up to full
sun radiating the perfumes of the skins,
to reach an accommodation inside. Everyone
hunts for water, starlings fly off with the take
and a shelter in which to sweat to
decant the body. The needs are basic,
underestimated by rhetorics of tools;
in a metal racket, or tubal web, lying
around with yellow or red in the face,
we wish we could shelter in each other,
give up our lives and keep
our inveterate longing spirits: embodied
like ash in a pan. Such openings give
permission to dream of perpetuity,
the shade falls at your feet like a saline dressing
how I fall out and in, marking the stages.
Simply a place to live, distances to mark
on a surface more forgiving than the sky
of every spot we chose, swept out and bounded
we still were far enough from intent
to keep trying that legacy of flesh.

THE HUSBAND

Inhale. Never to die happier and posting
this tenuous climax for dry futures, but here
intaglio skins never shed this resin etching
or series of gelatine prints all screwed into
the particular faces of the infants: demand
fostered by infusion of its negatives. Never to feel
that anxiety, all but dying squeezed out
of the decorator's tip into ripples, never to ask
for anything less than a box of matches
all laced in black diamonds in a pavé setting;
never to ask if I have to take my socks off,
never to open the lungs again unaccompanied.
All are there, all the mathematical animals
the subtracting monkeys and the interrogational
anteater with his electric probe: all around the house
scraping, scraping, all bent on escaping back into
the garden to use its fantastic implements.
Notice that snapped rosemary branch, some trodden
hyacinth and the patch of chlorosis. We are never
alone, we cannot exclude
the terrific persons or the index of leading shares
but how solitary one could have been, thinking so.
Even this shelter negating so many, so much
damage by exposure – she couldn't last it – and what
it contains leaks from some unsealed windows, some white
caught by some surveillance van working for the council.
The house which is warm boxlike paid for the house
of our children and our faithfulness, our marriage.
Comes down to one. Down to one, and in that one cove
and one ability and one constant streaming signal
make another one, at least another one. One
or two, or two and three
confused, narcissistic, appealing, right
turning faces the morbid animals, the straight tree
sipping its sap as a prognostication,

the crunching credit, the credit monsters relying
all on each other eating some and paying some others,
turning into the house, turning towards the windows,
holding up the couple. Holding the child up, the look out.
We will stay here until we die and never collapse
in awe at our great fortune, to subtract from all
the some who might help or hinder who defer our credit
rating, to elicit the negative and keep the image
blinding in its white heat against the irradiated night:
so absolute the fidelity to the track, the cut, the original,
do you hear a noise? It is nothing, the safe house
is bound in weather, we can rest in it together. We are
together, the continuum is our happiness, our troubles
the condition of possibility without retreat: no, no less
than everything, put on
the all in one, we being some who resound
in one range in the house knocking like a cooker, sing, chose
what one we want and wearing that to death. Exhale,
that can be your contribution to the world
the dangerous commerce. Sung twice over. We can do this,
let's do this, together. Look, there. Hear it? There. Exhale then, do it now.

DAMAGED GOOD

In the clearing smoke scours
the photographs, hiding the animal
labour which moves insects and their
information all over the face of the earth.

I arrive in kind by light rail
transport rough and undependable, rocking
sideways with a peg of metal to make
it ring eratogenically like spraypaint in a cylinder.
And get my tag up on the boundary stone.

Off the peg on the make, blush to be
at ease among gillyflowers where I toss
suffering to be carried back by animals,
the cabbage moth, the ordinary bee.

Chances start out anthological, and are re-
distributed by rationing: for loss looks better
and is altogether better an ethic. I am who
ties together the navigation menu
all the compassed interests of Variety
all three corners of the fading earth.

Watch all day the screen in ratio, facing
its light and movement with more affect
and concentration than the branching
face of a lover, as these spaces slip into degrees.
Two move along their loaned specificity
keep an eye on the melancholic
hourglass, poised beside the leftward arrow,
of the machine asking us to wait some more.

We share one hope, and it infuses even
the green-lipped mussel we eat sickly, the curl
of green-fringing kale. It bolts up the sky

and our assertion that there will be a future
clearing the smoke swings from its rootless peg.
That the blood will root, and take turns
through all the living work done on the earth
to divide and return to us intact. Ours is
the most abstract, and furthest from the truth.

REALITY STREET titles in print

Poetry series

Kelvin Corcoran: *Lyric Lyric* (1993)
Maggie O'Sullivan: *In the House of the Shaman* (1993)
Allen Fisher: *Dispossession and Cure* (1994)
Fanny Howe: *O'Clock* (1995)
Maggie O'Sullivan (ed.): *Out of Everywhere* (1996)
Cris Cheek/Sianed Jones: *Songs From Navigation* (1997)
Lisa Robertson: *Debbie: An Epic* (1997)
Maurice Scully: *Steps* (1997)
Denise Riley: *Selected Poems* (2000)
Lisa Robertson: *The Weather* (2001)
Robert Sheppard: *The Lores* (2003)
Lawrence Upton *Wire Sculptures* (2003)
Ken Edwards: *eight + six* (2003)
David Miller: *Spiritual Letters (I-II)* (2004)
Redell Olsen: *Secure Portable Space* (2004)
Peter Riley: *Excavations* (2004)
Allen Fisher: *Place* (2005)
Tony Baker: *In Transit* (2005)
Jeff Hilson: *stretchers* (2006)
Maurice Scully: *Sonata* (2006)
Maggie O'Sullivan: *Body of Work* (2006)
Sarah Riggs: *chain of minuscule decisions in the form of a feeling* (2007)
Carol Watts: *Wrack* (2007)
Jeff Hilson (ed.): *The Reality Street Book of Sonnets* (2008)
Peter Jaeger: *Rapid Eye Movement* (2009)
Wendy Mulford: *The Land Between* (2009)
Allan K Horwitz/Ken Edwards (ed.): *Botsotso* (2009)
Bill Griffiths: *Collected Earlier Poems* (2010)
Fanny Howe: *Emergence* (2010)
Jim Goar: *Seoul Bus Poems* (2010)
James Davies: *Plants* (2011)
Carol Watts: *Occasionals* (2011)
Paul Brown: *A Cabin in the Mountains* (2012)
Maggie O'Sullivan: *Waterfalls* (2012)
Peter Hughes: *Allotment Architecture* (2013)

Narrative series

Ken Edwards: *Futures* (1998, reprinted 2010)
John Hall: *Apricot Pages* (2005)
David Miller: *The Dorothy and Benno Stories* (2005)
Douglas Oliver: *Whisper 'Louise'* (2005)
Ken Edwards: *Nostalgia for Unknown Cities* (2007)
Paul Griffiths: *let me tell you* (2008)
John Gilmore: *Head of a Man* (2011)
Richard Makin: *Dwelling* (2011)
Leopold Haas: *The Raft* (2011)
Johan de Wit: *Gero Nimo* (2011)
David Miller (ed.): *The Alchemist's Mind* (2012)
Sean Pemberton: *White* (2012)
Ken Edwards: *Down With Beauty* (2013)
Philip Terry: *tapestry* (2013)

For updates on titles in print, a listing of out-of-print titles, and to order Reality Street books, please go to www.realitystreet.co.uk. For any other enquiries, email info@realitystreet.co.uk or write to the address on the reverse of the title page.

REALITY STREET depends for its continuing existence on the Reality Street Supporters scheme. For details of how to become a Reality Street Supporter, or to be put on the mailing list for news of forthcoming publications, write to the address on the reverse of the title page, or email **info@realitystreet.co.uk**

Visit our website at: **www.realitystreet.co.uk/supporter-scheme.php**

Reality Street Supporters who have sponsored this book:

Alan Baker
Andrew Brewerton
Peter Brown
Paul Buck
Clive Bush
Mark Callan
John Cayley
Adrian Clarke
Dane Cobain
Mary Coghill
Kelvin Corcoran
Ian Davidson
David Dowker
Carrie Etter
Gareth Farmer
Allen Fisher/Spanner
Penny Florence
Hilary Fraser
Sarah Gall
John Goodby
Paul Griffiths
Chris Gutkind
Charles Hadfield
Catherine Hales
John Hall
Alan Halsey
Robert Hampson
Tania Hershman
Gad Hollander
Simon Howard
Fanny Howe
Peter Hughes

Romana Huk
Elizabeth James
Keith Jebb
L Kiew
Peter Larkin
Sang-Yeon Lee/Jim Goar
Richard Leigh
Tony Lopez
Chris Lord
Richard Makin
Michael Mann
Lisa Mansell
Peter Manson
Ian Mcewen
Ian McMillan
Geraldine Monk
Pete & Lyn
Dennis Phillips
Tom Quale
Josh Robinson
Lou Rowan
Will Rowe
Jason Skeet
Valerie & Geoffrey Soar
Alan Teder
Philip Terry
Paul Vangelisti
Juha Virtanen
Susan Wheeler
John Wilkinson
Johan de Wit
Anonymous: 4